THE HOME UNIVERSITY LIBRARY
OF MODERN KNOWLEDGE

· 104 ·

POLITICAL THOUGHT
IN ENGLAND
1848 to 1914

POLITICAL THOUGHT
IN ENGLAND
1848 to 1914

ERNEST BARKER

GREENWOOD PRESS, PUBLISHERS
WESTPORT, CONNECTICUT

Library of Congress Cataloging in Publication Data

Barker, Ernest, Sir, 1874-1960.
  Political thought in England, 1848 to 1914.

    Reprint of the 1945 issue of the 2d ed. (1928)
  published by Oxford University Press, London, New York,
  which was issued as no. 104 of the Home university
  library of modern knowledge.
    Bibliography: p.
    Includes index.
    1. Political science--Great Britain--History.
  I. Title.
  JA84.G7B3 1980   320'.0941   80-19766
  ISBN 0-313-22216-9 (lib. bdg.)

First published in 1915 under title: Political Thought in
England from Herbert Spencer to the Present Day. This is a
reprint of the 1945 reissue of the second edition, 1928.

This reprint has been authorized by the Oxford University Press.

Reprinted in 1980 by Greenwood Press
A division of Congressional Information Service, Inc.
88 Post Road West, Westport, Connecticut 06881

Printed in the United States of America

10 9 8 7 6 5 4 3 2 1

CONTENTS

PREFACE TO THE REPRINT OF 1945

THIS is a reprint, with some few changes in the last few pages, of the original book as it was published thirty years ago, during the early months of the War of 1914–18. No attempt has been made to 'bring it up to date', or to revise the verdicts passed by the author in what now seems a different age—an age when politics were domestic politics, and peace still seemed the habit of life. A Thirty Years War—one-third of it open, and two-thirds raging beneath the surface—has darkened the skies since the book was written. Revision will one day be needed—if the book and its author still live; but revision must wait until some vantage-point has been reached from which it is possible to look back, in the light (as it were) of the darkness through which we have passed, and to see the true significance of the period of thought which preceded the storm.

Meanwhile there may still be some value in a record, put together just at its close, and couched in its terms (which are not necessarily antiquated), of the phase of English political thought which lasted from 1848 to 1914. There is an interest in remembering what we were thinking when the storm broke; and a view of the period, taken just at its close, different as it may be from the view which would now be taken by an author writing 'thirty years after', has perhaps some sort of historical value. At any rate the reader, riper by a whole generation of experience than the writer was when he wrote this book, will be able to judge how far he spoke prudently, and how far at random, about the current tendencies, and the future possibilities, of political thought in England on the eve of the Thirty Years War.

ERNEST BARKER

17 CRANMER ROAD
CAMBRIDGE
April 1945

vi

POLITICAL THOUGHT IN ENGLAND

CHAPTER I

INTRODUCTION

THE year 1848 was the *annus mirabilis* of the nineteenth century. A whole continent was in travail with new nationalities and new constitutions. If in England the days of that eventful year ran more quietly, they were nevertheless stirring. There were no " national workshops " in London, and English workmen claimed no " right to work "; but at any rate Mill's *Principles of Political Economy* appeared, and the prophet of individualism was found to be drawing a distinction between the laws of production and the laws of distribution, which opened the gates for the entry of Socialism. The Chartist movement came to an abortive end; but the Christian Socialists attempted to found a co-operative movement, and in 1850 Kingsley published *Alton Locke*. A new school appeared in English art. While Thackeray was finishing *Vanity Fair*, and Macaulay was publishing the first two volumes of his *History of England*, a brotherhood was being formed by Holman Hunt, Rossetti and Millais, and the Pre-Raphaelite movement was being born. Ten years later, in 1858, the doctrine of

7

Natural Selection was enunciated; and a new and powerful leaven was added to the fermentation of ideas already at work in the general mind.

Men began to feel the need of a more scientific explanation of the facts, and a more scientific attempt to cure the defects, of social life. Two revolutions had passed over the world in the last few decades—the political revolution which had started in France in 1789, and the industrial revolution which had begun in England about 1760. The fruits of the one had still to be garnered : the unforeseen results of the other had still to be faced. On the one hand, the political demands of the Chartists had to be met with some reasonable answer; and statesmen had to determine how far, and by what means, the French doctrine of the sovereignty of *volonté générale* should be incorporated into the parliamentary system and electoral machinery of England. On the other hand, sterner and more exacting, there loomed the massive problem of the " condition of England." With the eye of genius Disraeli had already seized and stated the problem in *Sybil ;* with the sympathy of a philanthropist Shaftesbury had already begun to attempt some solution. A new force, partly a complication of the problem, partly, and indeed mainly, a help and a way of solution, had appeared in the Trade Unions, which had now, for some twenty years or more, been freed by the efforts of Francis Place from the shackles of the Combination Laws. Meanwhile the English Church, under the stimulus of the

Oxford Movement, had awakened since 1833 to a new sense of its own corporate life; and devoted churchmen, conscious of the duty of their Society to its members, were turning to those social activities which have ever since marked the work of the High Church party in England.

The accepted creed, which had to face these new problems and tendencies, was a creed proceeding from Adam Smith and Jeremy Bentham. Formed at a time when the " policy of Europe " still choked the channels of trade, and feudal survivals still encumbered the laws and filled with " sinister interests " the governments of Europe, that creed had been a corrosive solvent of everything that clogged the free play of individual activity. But times were changed, and the creed was also changed with the times. It had condemned governmental interference in the name alike of economic and political liberty; it continued to condemn governmental interference, when such condemnation could only serve the cause of social oppression. Liberty for the manufacturer and the seller was not necessarily liberty for the worker : it was indeed only too often the very reverse; and a modification of the old philosophy of human action, if not an entirely new philosophy, was an urgent necessity, if social progress was not to be checked by a social creed. A modification, partly conscious and partly unconscious, appeared in the writings of John Stuart Mill, one of the finest minds and most generous natures of the nineteenth century. In the *Essay On Liberty* he gave a deeper and more spiritual

A 2

interpretation to the conception of liberty. From a conception of liberty as external freedom of action, necessary for the discovery and pursuit of his material interest by each individual, Mill rose to the conception of liberty as free play for that spiritual originality, with all its results in " individual vigour and manifold diversity," which alone can constitute a rich, balanced and developed society. In a similar way, in the *Essay On Representative Government*, he spiritualised the Benthamite defence of democracy. Instead of regarding popular self-government as freedom for the people to pursue its own self-interest at the expense of the " sinister interests " of classes and sections, he conceived representative institutions as the necessary condition of that individual energy of mind and character which must be developed all round and in all things, and can only be so developed if the area of individual thought and will is extended to embrace the affairs of the whole community. His philosophy found room for Trade Unions, a form of voluntary association which gave scope for liberty; it even admitted the possibility of social regulation of the laws of distribution. Yet when all these allowances are made, it still remains true that Mill was the prophet of an empty liberty and an abstract individual. He had no clear philosophy of rights, through which alone the conception of liberty attains a concrete meaning; he had no clear idea of that social whole in whose realisation the false antithesis of " state " and " individual " disappears.

Not a modification of the old Benthamite

premisses, but a new philosophy was needed; and that philosophy was provided by the idealist school, of which Green is the greatest representative. That school drew its inspiration immediately from Kant and Hegel, and ultimately from the old Greek philosophy of the city-state. The vital relation between the life of the individual and the life of the community, which alone gives the individual worth and significance, because it alone gives him the power of full moral development; the dependence of the individual, for all his rights and for all his liberty, on his membership of the community; the correlative duty of the community to guarantee to the individual all his rights (in other words all the conditions necessary for his, and therefore for its own, full moral development)—these were the premisses of the new philosophy. That philosophy could satisfy the new needs of social progress, because it refused to worship a supposed individual liberty which was proving destructive of the real liberty of the vast majority, and preferred to emphasise the moral well-being and betterment of the whole community, and to conceive of each of its members as attaining his own well-being and betterment in and through the community. Herein lay, or seemed to lie, a revolution of ideas. Instead of starting from a central individual, to whom the social system is supposed to be adjusted, the idealist starts from a central social system, in which the individual must find his appointed orbit of duty. But after all the revolution is only a restoration; and what is restored is simply the *Republic* of Plato.

Political philosophy not only advances of itself, and through its own acquisition of new, or restatement of old, philosophic conceptions; it also advances through the contributions of other studies, which can either supply analogies to guide its method or new facts to increase its content. Political philosophy in itself, and apart from other studies, is essentially an ethical study, which regards the State as a moral society, and inquires into the ways by which it seeks to attain its ultimate moral aim. Assuming a moral ideal for all human institutions, and therefore for the State as one of the greatest of these institutions, political philosophy interprets the State in terms of ethics, and seeks to determine its relation to the moral constitution and development of man. But other studies may influence its method, or add to its content. Mathematics, for instance, may suggest, as it suggested to Comte, a method for "social science," which will make it as much concerned with "laws," and as much capable of prediction, as any of the physical sciences; and history may suggest an historical method, which will turn inquiry towards the genesis of social institutions, and will seek to explain the *raison d'être* of such institutions from the recorded facts of their life and action. More important are those studies which can add to the content of social philosophy. These studies are necessarily studies of man, and more particularly of man in some social aspect, in which he stands related to his fellows. Two such studies in particular, both peculiarly English, at any rate in their beginnings, have influenced political theory in England during the last sixty years. These are biology and political economy. A third study, in which inspiration has largely been drawn from Germany, but in which native elements may also be traced, has also reacted on English political theory. This is the study of jurisprudence. Still another study—that of psychology, more particularly on its social side—has been increasingly applied, first in France, then in America, and of late years also in England, to the elucidation and interpretation of social phenomena. Finally, historical studies, whether directed, as they are by historians proper, to the growth of civilisation, or turned, as they are by anthropologists, to times and spaces that lie behind civilisation, have not only suggested a new method, but have also added new data to the study of social philosophy. Biology, political economy, jurisprudence, psychology, history, are all studies which, though they lie in different fields from social philosophy proper, nevertheless deal with a subject-matter that is connected with and acts upon the peculiar subject-matter of social philosophy. The moral nature of man is isolated in no vacuum; it stands in intimate and organic relation with physical structure and economic motive, with legal enactment, with social instinct, with historic or pre-historic institutions. Such relations social philosophy must necessarily consider. What it cannot admit is that any of the studies which deal with these other matters can solely or even primarily explain the reason and the value of society. They can throw additional light on the ultimate

moral factor; in themselves they are necessarily one-sided and therefore misleading
guides. They cannot absolve us from the
primary duty of studying the State as the product and organ of the moral will of men.

It was natural that political economy, the
most peculiarly English study, and the study
most closely allied to political theory, should
influence that theory most profoundly. Such
influence has been operative in two opposite
directions. On the one hand the old " classical " political economy of Adam Smith and
Ricardo has tended to make laissez-faire a
political dogma; on the other hand newer
versions of political economy, largely springing
from Germany—whether the nationalist pro-
tectionism of List, or the international socialism of Marx—have made for state-interference
on an ever-increasing scale. Much the same
would seem to be true of biology. It is a study
which has owed much to English thinkers;
it is a study which whether by the analogies
which it supplies, such as that of the physical
organism, or the new facts it presents, such as
those of struggle for life and survival of the
fittest, readily exercises a considerable influence on political theory. Its influence, like
that of political economy, has been operative
in two opposite directions. On the one hand
Herbert Spencer, though holding the idea of
a social organism, somewhat inconsistently
dissolved that idea into an antithesis of " the
man *versus* the state," and claimed the utmost
liberty for the individual; on the other hand
biologists of a later date, influenced by the
idea of hereditary transmission of qualities and

defects, seem prepared to enlist the State in
aid of natural selection, and to bring eugenics,
as Socialists would bring economics, under a
measure of political control.

The connection between jurisprudence and
political theory is close and obvious. If the
one is concerned with justice, and the other
with morality—if the one deals with the external rules which direct actions in an ordered
community, and the other with the ideas that
lie behind rules and the ideal which lies behind
order—both are at any rate concerned with
the relations one to another of men who are
living in communities. For many centuries,
indeed, while the doctrine of the Social Contract ruled the schools, the conceptions and
the terminology of jurisprudence dominated
political theory. Nor has the old alliance
been altogether broken in England since 1848.
Maine popularised Savigny's conception of
law as a continuous historical development,
and used that conception to undermine the
doctrine of aboriginal natural rights; and he
was ultimately led by his historical feeling
towards that conservative tendency which
had made Savigny oppose the plan for a
codification of German law, and which made
Maine himself look coldly and critically on
democracy in his *Popular Government.* Law
may indeed seem to many of us to be at all
times a conservative influence; yet it was law
which produced the radical doctrine of the
Social Contract, and it is law, as interpreted
by Maitland, which has of late years added
new and radical ideas to the content of political theory. Following Gierke, Maitland

has vindicated the real personality, the spontaneous origin, the inherent rights of corporate bodies within the State, and he has thus suggested lines of thought favourable to the claims of Trade Unions, of Churches, and of other organised bodies which live within the limits of the State. Meanwhile, a more peculiarly English tradition has been represented by Dicey, who has interpreted for us the legal meaning of our own constitution, and investigated the currents of opinion which have contributed to determine the course of our recent legislation.

If law is a study of what we may call objective mind—of mind as concrete and embodied in external rules and sanctions—psychology seeks to study those inner processes of mind which lie behind law and all social conduct. Such processes, under the name of " imitation " and " social logic," have been investigated more especially by French thinkers like Tarde; and something of their method and ideas has descended upon those English sociologists, like MacDougall and Graham Wallas, who seek to find in psychology the key to social phenomena. The defect of such a line of approach lies in the tendency which it encourages to regard a close analysis of social phenomena (and that is all which psychology can give) as identical with something of a very different order—the explanation of the why and wherefore of those phenomena. To analyse the processes of social instinct that lie in the dim background of a society now united in the pursuit of a common moral object is not to explain the real nature or the real cause of such a society. It is only to describe genesis; and Aristotle long ago emphasised the difference between the physical (one may add the psycho-physical) processes, which explain the genesis of the State, and the moral reasons which explain its existence, when he spoke of the State as arising in the needs of mere life, but existing through the necessities of a moral life. The same tendency to turn mere temporal priority into causal relation is equally encouraged by the application of the historical method to political theory. Maine did solid work, when from the evidence of ancient law he sought to exhibit the origins of early society, and anthropologists by new methods and the use of new data have added to the work he began. We must admit the value of the new data thus provided; we must allow that the continuity of human life is brought home to us, when we can thus trace the roots of the present in the past, and discover in tribal societies the germs of that moral person which we call the State. But we must also recognise that Maine did not explode the theory of the Social Contract— a theory intended to explain not the temporal antecedents but the logical presuppositions of the State—when he proved that history is marked by a sequence of events proceeding not *from* contract, but *to* contract; and we must remember with Hobbes that philosophy " excludes history as well natural as political, though most useful (nay, necessary) to philo-sophy; because such knowledge is but ex-perience, and not ratiocination."

To discover the immanent political philosophy of the last sixty years we have thus not only to study the works they have produced in social philosophy; we have also to consider the contributions of method, of data, of outlook, from biology and political economy, from law and history, from psychology and anthropology. Nor is this all. Our men of letters—Carlyle and Ruskin and Matthew Arnold; our novelists—Dickens and Reade and Kingsley; our dramatists, like Shaw and Galsworthy, have thought and written not a little of social and political matters. It may almost be said that the " sophistic " trend of our age—its impulse towards a drastic criticism and revision of conventional morality—finds its best representative in the drama. Finally, beyond all this writing in all these spheres, we must remember the vast area of oral discussion, which our party system involves. Herein, indeed, we may see the cause, as well as the content, of much of our theorising. On the one hand party causes theories to spring into the arena; or at any rate party enlists theories to fight its battles. On the other hand, the programme of a party is an embodied theory : its measures are the concrete expression in organically interrelated detail of a way of looking at political life. From the one point of view we may notice the philosophy of Bergson enlisted by the Syndicalist party; or we may notice the theory of Gierke pressed into service both by defenders of Trade Unionism and by those High Churchmen who argue for the independence of ecclesiastical societies. From the other point of view we may watch the Socialist party working out gradually a concrete theory of Socialism; or we may watch the Liberal party seeking to embody in legislation a more positive theory of liberty than the Benthamite school had attained. It is true that there always tend to be unresolved elements in the programme of a party, which cannot be logically connected with its underlying theory, but are either inheritances from a past otherwise sloughed, or concessions to the needs of the hour and the demands of interested supporters. None the less we must recognise that the programme of a party tends to embody a set of measures which are organically interdependent, because they express in detail a single set of conceptions.

So far we have considered the different lines of approach to political theory—whether through ethics or through natural science, through economics or through law—which have been attempted during the whole of the period under survey. The line of division has been logical rather than chronological. If we turn to consider the development of political speculation chronologically, we find that it falls into definite periods. From 1848 to 1880 the general tendency is towards individualism. The policy of laissez-faire finds general acceptance. Laissez-faire means on the one hand, and in domestic politics, a restriction of governmental activity to the bare minimum: on the other hand, and in foreign affairs, a policy of free trade and of friendship between nations. Spencer is the thoroughgoing prophet of laissez-faire, from *Social*

Statics (1850) at one end to *The Man Versus the State* (1885) at the other. He provides individualism with a coat of natural science; he presses into its service the antithesis between militarism and industrialism, and urges that the natural process of evolution has made laissez-faire the guiding principle of the modern epoch of industry. John Stuart Mill is less thorough-going. He is a transitional force; and in his hands utilitarianism begins to be less individualistic, and assumes more and more a socialistic quality. Social utility, he thinks, is the goal; to this, he feels, it may be the supreme duty of the individual to sacrifice himself; for this, he allows, it may be necessary to entrust the State with large functions of controlling the distribution of wealth. Meanwhile the influence of literature, preeminently in Carlyle and Ruskin, is directed vehemently against laissez-faire and all its works—works at once unjust in the eyes of the moralist and unlovely in the eyes of the artist. In place of the doctrine of " go-as-you-like " Carlyle and Ruskin urge the need of guidance and governance; they plead for the rule of the wise, and for the regulation and regimentation, even on military lines, of the life and action of the community.

By 1880 the doctrine of laissez-faire—the preaching of non-intervention as the supreme duty of the State, internally as well as externally—seems to have passed. It had not only been undermined by the literary prophets : facts themselves were against it. Since 1870 the State had been concerning itself seriously with education; and still

further extensions of its powers were being
made inevitable by the crying needs of the
time.   By 1880 Green is lecturing at Oxford
on *The Principles of Political Obligation*, and
arguing that the State must intervene to
remove all obstacles which impede the free
moral development of its citizens.   Soon after
1880 Socialism is established in England in
both its forms.   The revolutionary Socialism
of the type of Hyndman is advocating the
introduction of a socialist régime *en bloc*, and
preaching the Class-War as the necessary pre-
lude : the reformist Socialism of the Fabians
is advocating the gradual conquest of one reform after another, and preaching the method
of permeation of all classes ; but both alike are
urging society to take into its hands the control
of its economic life.   The guidance and governance which Carlyle had desired seemed to be
imminent, though they were not to proceed
from that aristocracy of the wise which he had
expected to be their source.   Men of the old
school began to be alarmed, particularly when
the franchise was extended in 1884; and
Spencer turned to defend the individual once
more against the encroachments of the State,
while Maine in *Popular Government* grew pessimistic over the advancing flood of democracy.

Just when theory and practice alike seemed
to presage a large growth of the intervention
of the State in internal affairs, the whole process seemed to be checked by the " imperialist
reaction."   But it is perhaps a mistake to
talk of " reaction."   There was not in reality
a check to the growth of intervention.   Intervention grew, but it was external rather

than internal. In any case laissez-faire, with its doctrine of a foreign policy based on pacific cosmopolitanism, steadily lost ground. From 1884 to 1903 vast territories, mainly in Africa, but partly also in Asia, were added to the Empire; and a wide-spread political theory, which it is true hardly found any representative voice, began to preach " the white man's burden." It would be futile to assign this movement to any peculiarly English cause. When we reflect that France and to a lesser degree Germany were increasing or founding colonial empires at the same time, we must acknowledge that the cause is general and European. If we seek such a cause, we can only find it, apart from economic motives, which are generally exaggerated, in the idea of Nationalism—that exclusive nationalism, which till of late possessed England, and now possesses Germany, and whose essence it is, as has been finely said, " that the members of each nation believe their national civilisation to be Civilisation."

Collectivism had wrought to exalt the province of the State : Nationalism seems to have entered and reaped the crop which it had sown. But at any rate one side of laissez-faire—the policy of external non-intervention, of peace and retrenchment of armaments—disappeared soon after 1880. Since 1903 the complementary domestic policy, which had entered the stage in 1870, has assumed a leading part. It matters little that one party has espoused the cause of protection, and the other the cause of social reform. Both parties are " interventionists " in domestic, as both

parties, in a greater or less degree, are interventionists in foreign policy.   The difference
between the general tone and temper of 1864
and the tone and temper 1914—the difference,
if we take a rough line of division, between the
generation before and the generation after
1880—is profound.   While in 1864 orthodoxy
meant distrust of the State, and heresy took
the form of a belief in paternal government,
in 1914 orthodoxy means belief in the
State, and heresy takes the form of mild
excursions into anarchism.   The most recent
philosophies, whether propounded in a legal
form, as by Maitland, or in the form of social
economics, as by syndicalists and believers in
guild-socialism, are directed towards the vindication of the independence of groups.   The
modern anarchist, in revolt against an excess
of government, does not, like Auberon Herbert
or   Wordsworth   Donisthorpe,   preach   the
principle of " Let Be " for the benefit of the
individual : he preaches it for the benefit of
the organised group, and particularly of the
organised profession or guild.   But it is non-
intervention, if in a new form, which is again
being inculcated as the rule for the internal
policy of the State.   How far its external
policy is likely to be modified in the same
direction, the future alone will show.

CHAPTER II

THE IDEALIST SCHOOL—T. H. GREEN

THE idealist philosophy of the State,
which is set forth in the writings of Green,

Bradley and Bosanquet, is largely a product
of Oxford. Among the sources of this philosophy we must give the first place to the study
of the Greek Classics. The influence of
Plato and Aristotle has been peculiarly deep
in England. The curriculum of the oldest and
most important branch of studies in Oxford
finds in the *Republic* of Plato and the *Ethics*
of Aristotle its central texts; and truths
drawn from Greek thought have been learned
in Oxford, and enforced in the world, not
only by the thinkers, but also by the men of
action, who have been trained in this curriculum. Generations of students have learned
from Plato and Aristotle the lessons that
" man by the law of his being is a member
of a political community "; that the true
State is a " partnership in a life of virtue ";
that law is the expression of pure and
passionless reason; that righteousness consists
for each man in the fulfilment of his appointed
function in the life and action of the community. These lessons have not been forgotten. " If you take English political
thought and action from Pitt and Fox onwards," writes Prof. Murray, " it seems to
me that you will always find present . . .
strands of feeling which are due—of course
among many other causes—to this germination of Greek influence; an unquestioning
respect for freedom of life and thought, a
mistrust of passion . . . a sure consciousness
that the poor are the fellow citizens of the
rich, and that statesmen must as a matter
of fact consider the welfare of the whole
State."

The ultimate basis of the idealist philosophy of the State is thus to be found in the writings of Plato and Aristotle, and in a steady tradition of study and teaching of the *Republic* and the *Ethics*. Another and more immediate influence is that of German philosophy. Green drew his inspiration from Kant and Hegel as well as from Plato and Aristotle. And in fact the philosophical theory of the State, of which Green and Bosanquet are the chief representatives, is a commentary and exposition, an expansion and modification, of the political philosophy first expounded in Germany at the end of the eighteenth and the beginning of the nineteenth century.

In developing their theories both Kant and Hegel start from Rousseau's conception of moral freedom as the peculiar and distinctive quality of man, and both consider the State entirely in its relation to this freedom. With Kant, however—this at any rate was Hegel's criticism—freedom has a negative, limited and subjective meaning, which makes his attitude to the State somewhat grudging and individualistic. Kant interpreted freedom as the right to will a self-imposed imperative of duty, and he insisted that every man, possessing in virtue of his reason such a will, existed, and ought to be used, always as an end in himself and never as merely a means. To Hegel freedom of this kind is negative because it wears the face of duty, and it is limited because it isolates each man as an end in himself. Such freedom, again, is subjective, because it resides in the inner world of intention and conscience, and does not find a free

issue outwards into objective life. By what
gate, then, does the conception of the State
enter into the political philosophy of Kant?
Fundamentally, perhaps, through the conception of duty as something in its nature universal. The individual who wills the imperative
of duty is willing something which, if it
applies to the particular occasion, is at the
same time a universal. When he lays down
the rule *Thou shalt not steal*, he is really con-
stituting a general rule, and ultimately,
because he builds a whole system of such
rules, he is creating a set of laws which must
necessarily be enshrined in and enforced by a
State. But the more simple and obvious
answer which Kant gives to the question
seems to be found in the conception of contract. By contract men " surrender their
external freedom in order to receive it immediately back again as members of a commonwealth "; they " abandon their wild lawless
freedom in order to substitute a perfect
freedom—a freedom undiminished, because it
is the creation of their own free legislative
will; but a freedom which nevertheless
assumes the form of a lawful dependence, because it takes its place in a realm of Right or
Law." Kant, it appears, had little idea of
the corporate life of a national State. The
free will of the individual is the core of his
thought. The State he conceives as in its
nature a contractual body; and far from
exalting the control of the State over the
individual, he emphasises the necessary sub-
ordination of the State to the ideal of a permanent peace of Europe, and advocates a federal

league of nations, each subject to the adjudication of the general collective will.

Hegel, in opposition to Kant, sketched a more positive and objective conception of freedom, and a less individualistic conception of the State. Freedom, he holds, must be positive. It is expansion: it consists in the will to make my outward self adequate to the measure of the fulness of my thinking self. For this reason, freedom must also be objective, or outwardly expressed. It is creative: it expresses itself in a series of outward manifestations—first the law; then the rules of inward morality; and finally the whole system of institutions and influences that make for righteousness in the national State. That system of institutions and influences Hegel embraces in the term Social Ethics (*Sittlichkeit*); and in Social Ethics he finds the reconciliation of the mere externality of law and the mere inwardness of morality. By this means Hegel achieved a view of the State less individualistic than that of Kant appeared to him to be. In the State man has fully raised his outward self to the level of the inward self of thought: his free will has found the broadest expansion which its positive quality demands, and the highest expression which its objective character requires. To such a State no idea of contract can apply: contract belongs to the domain of mere law, and is only concerned with property. The State must be envisaged in terms neither of law nor of the morality of individual conscience, but in terms of social ethics. It is an expression, and the highest expression, of that social morality,

at once precipitated in and enforced by social
opinion, which lies behind the life of the family,
behind the life of all other social groups, and
behind the life of the political community
itself. That social morality is the product of a
free will seeking to realise itself in a positive
and objective form; and the State, as the
highest expression and organ of social morality,
is therefore also the product of that will—a
product not in the sense of a definite creation,
at a given point of time, but in the sense of
something gradually evolved, yet implicit all
the time. Produced by the free will, the State
sustains it—and this by a double function.
In the first place it maintains the individual as
a person, and not only maintains him, but
promotes his welfare and protects the minor
groups of family and social life in which he
partially seeks his welfare : in the second
place, " it carries back . . . the individual—
whose tendency it is to become a centre of his
own—into the life of the universal substance."
In a word, it sustains personality, and it
teaches personality to transcend itself by
giving its devotion to something beyond
itself. Thus Hegel is brought to a belief in the
divinity of the nation. Two influences combined to produce this belief. One was the
influence of the Greek city-state, with its
theory that the individual exists in order to
perform his allotted function in the life of the
community, and that " none of the citizens
belongs to himself, since they all belong to the
State." In his *System of Ethics* of 1802, his
earliest deliverance in the field of political
theory, Hegel already shows himself imbued

with the ideals of the Greek past. The other
influence was that of contemporary national
feeling. The rush and the sweep of the French
Revolution of 1789 had stimulated every
political thinker; it had helped to inspire
Kant's theory of freedom, and perhaps served
to suggest his ideal of permanent peace. At
a later date, after 1812, the national reaction
against Napoleon had led men to realise that
the national State has a hold on men's hearts
and allegiance, which cannot be explained by
any notion of contract, and for which only the
idea of the real and personal existence of the
nation can serve to account. Hegel lived in
these later days, and he was led by their
influence to exalt the national State to a
mystical height. But this lofty mysticism has,
naturally if paradoxically, its somewhat tragic
results. On the one hand Hegel holds that the
unity of the State, " the free power that interferes with subordinate spheres," must be
incorporated in " an actual individual, in the
will of a decreeing individual, in monarchy."
On the other hand he permits the State, as the
highest expression of social morality, to escape
from any moral restrictions. " The state of
war," he writes, " shows the omnipotence of
the State in its individuality "; country and
fatherland are then the power, which convicts
of nullity the independence of individuals.

We shall see how Green departs from
Hegel's views in these last two phases—how
little he believes in absolute monarchy; how
much he believes in that international
morality, which Hegel too readily dismissed.
But before turning to English political theory,

we must notice that Hegel, and to some extent
even Kant, have little love for English institutions. Hegel attacks the representative institutions of England, which had generally been
regarded as ensuring to her citizens the freest
of constitutions; he argues that England is
really the most backward country in Europe,
because true freedom, which can only be
realised by monarchy, is sacrificed by the
English system of representative institutions
to private and particular interests. Even
Kant distrusts representative institutions,
though he is less full of the zeal for undivided
sovereignty than Hegel; he fears that representatives will tend to be unduly dependent on
ministers. Some modification of the theories
of Kant and Hegel is thus obviously needed to
make the idealist theory of the Continent
square with the representative institutions of
England, and to adjust a theory which emphasises the " majesty " of the State to a practice
which emphasises the " liberty of the subject."

The England in which Green developed his
political philosophy was the England of the
years after 1870. A change was then passing
over public opinion, and law was reflecting this
change. Legislation, in Prof. Dicey's phrase,
was passing from an individualist to a collectivist trend. The word "collectivist" is perhaps
a misnomer; but at any rate it is clear that
the State was no longer confining itself, if
indeed it ever had done, to securing the free
play of competition and vindicating freedom
of contract, but was addressing itself to the
more positive function, already foreshadowed
in the Factory Acts, of securing the conditions

of virtuous living for each and all of its members. Green, as much of a sober realist as of a soaring idealist, addressed himself to eliciting and explaining the presuppositions implicit in the contemporary life of the English State. He endeavoured, as his biographer says, " to awaken a consciousness of what man actually is and does in certain functions of his everyday life, this being, as he conceived, the true way to awaken the further consciousness of what he ought to be and do." By temper and experience of life he was eminently suited for his task. Tutor and afterwards professor in Oxford from 1860 to 1882, he was nevertheless no " academic " recluse. He had always a lively sympathy for the middle class and for nonconformity. He had, besides, a keen interest in education and licensing reform. In education he had always been interested from the time when, in 1856 and 1866, he was assistant commissioner to a royal commission on education; and he gave his time and his money to the foundation of a High School for Oxford boys. To the need of temperance reform his attention had early been drawn by his own experience of life; and in 1872 he joined the United Kingdom Alliance. In the civic politics of Oxford he took a share which has made his name a tradition and an example in the University. In national politics he was a Liberal of the school of John Bright; and from 1867 onwards he appeared on political platforms. One of the last of his writings was a lecture on *Liberal Legislation and Freedom of Contract*, which was given at Leicester in 1881 under the auspices of the Liberal Association of the town.

The *Lectures on the Principles of Political Obligation* were delivered by Green in the winter of 1879-1880, during his tenure of the chair of moral philosophy at Oxford. Of the ultimate metaphysical, or indeed, one may almost say, the ultimate religious principles which lay behind these lectures we cannot here give any account. But it must be remembered that behind his conception of the State lies the idea of an eternal self-consciousness, which communicates to human consciousness the idea of the social good, and to whose perfection, in turn, human consciousness is ever seeking to attain, and, in the higher forms of human society, has already partially attained. In the light of such an idea citizenship becomes Christian citizenship, and the State a *civitas Dei*. In the *Principles of Political Obligation*, however, it is from human consciousness, and from the liberty which that consciousness demands for itself, that the discourse starts.

The State is a product of this consciousness. Human consciousness postulates liberty : liberty involves rights : rights demand the State. All these terms, however, require definition. In taking our start from liberty, we should notice that Green begins from, always clings to, and finally ends in the Kantian doctrine of the free moral will in virtue of which man always wills himself as an end. The one thing of value is the good will. The one thing the State must not do is to check its self-determination, either by repressive interference or by paternal government : the one thing the State must do is to liberate its energies by removing the obstacles to their action. Liberty can only be liberty for this good will : it can only be liberty for the pursuit of the objects which such a will presents to itself. Liberty is therefore no negative absence of restraint, any more than beauty is the absence of ugliness. It is " a positive power of doing or enjoying something worth doing or enjoying." Liberty, again, inhering as it does in the good will, and in that will only, is not a power of pursuing any and every object, but a power of pursuing those objects which the good will presents to itself. In a word, it has two qualities. It is positive—a freedom to do something, not a freedom from having something done to one   It is determinate—a freedom to do something of a definite character, something which possesses the quality of being worth doing, and not any and everything.

Self-consciousness, then, postulates liberty. The self must not only know itself, but also will itself, in the sense of willing the ideal objects with which it has identified itself, or rather, is seeking to identify itself. But the self is not only conscious of itself; it is also conscious of other selves. Moreover, it is conscious of them as of like nature with itself— endowed with the same good will, and presenting to themselves the same objects. Therefore the " something done or enjoyed " must be " something that we do or enjoy in common with others." Nor is this all. The self not only wills the good of itself (such a conception of self is merely abstract and therefore unreal); it wills the goodness of itself in relation to others. It wills the goodness of its relations with others; it wills the goodness of the society

B

which is constituted by such relations. The goodness of the relations which constitute society means a system of rights. Under such a system each recognises in his fellow, and each claims from his fellow that he shall recognise in him, the power of pursuing ideal objects; and each makes his claim with a sure confidence of its recognition by all, because each is of like nature with his fellows, and the objects of all are common objects. Claims thus recognised are translated into rights, and it is such recognition that constitutes them rights. Thus, if we care to make the distinction, we may say that rights have a double aspect. On the one hand a right is the claim of an individual, arising from the nature of self-consciousness, for permission to will his own ideal objects; on the other hand it is the recognition of that claim by society and, therein and thereby, the addition of a new power to pursue these objects. Such a distinction has its value when we are dealing with inchoate rights—with such a condition, for instance, as that in North America before 1866, when freedom from slavery was claimed, but was not yet openly recognised by society. But really the distinction is abstract. All real rights imply and contain both aspects. Rights must inhere in individuals; but they can only inhere in them as members of a society which gives its recognition, and in virtue of the community of ideal objects which causes that recognition.

We must, however, be clear about the meaning of the word recognition. Green is not speaking of legal recognition : nor is he endorsing Bentham's dictum, that "rights properly so called are the creatures of law properly so called." The rights with which he is concerned are not legal rights, but ideal rights : they are the rights which a society properly organised on the basis of the good will should ideally recognise, if it is true to its own basic principle. Such rights we may fairly term " natural " rights, if we conceive natural rights properly ; if we regard them, not in the old and erroneous way, as rights which isolated men possessed in a pre-social state of nature and must consequently be presumed (though the consequence is not obvious) to possess in a state of society, but as rights inherent and " innate " in the moral nature of associated men who are living (as they cannot but live) in some form of society. These ideal, or natural, rights are broader and deeper than actual or legal rights, which are, at any given moment in any given State, the expression, necessarily partial and incomplete, of the conception of natural rights attained by that State. We can now see that the rights of which Green speaks are relative to morality rather than law ; and the recognition of which he speaks is recognition by a common moral consciousness rather than by a legislature. The rights are relative to morality, in the sense that they are the conditions of the attainment of the moral end, and the recognition is given by the moral consciousness, because it knows that they are the necessary conditions of its own satisfaction. But though we may connect rights with morality, there is nevertheless a distinction to be drawn between the obligation to respect rights and the obligation to observe purely moral duties. The one obligation can be, and ultimately is, enforced by law; the other cannot. In the one case the recognition of the moral consciousness, when it is sufficiently general and sufficiently explicit—when " opinion is ripe "—passes into a law, with external sanctions attached to its breach : in the other case it never can. The ground for this distinction we shall see later, when we come to discuss the province of state-action. So far as we have gone, it is sufficient if we realise two things. On the one hand the rights of which Green speaks are so far related to law that they can be and ultimately are embodied in law; and they are so far related to morality that their value lies in their service to the moral end, and their source is to be found in the moral consciousness of man. On the other hand they are distinct from law, because the actual rights embodied in the actual law of a community never quite square with an ideal system; and they are distinct from morality, because they are enforceable (whether or no they are actually enforced) by external sanctions, and morality is not, and cannot be, thus enforced.[1]

Rights are enforceable, and indeed have to be enforced. Here we pass beyond the conception as yet attained—the conception of a society of selves, conscious of one another and conscious of a common end, and therefore recognising one another and the common end—

[1] " Law defines existing legal rights; Ethics defines moral rights; Politics defines those moral rights which would be legally enforceable if law were what it ought to be."—Jethro Brown, *Underlying Principles of Modern Legislation*, p. 192.

and we turn to speak of sovereignty, that is to say, of the power which enforces rights. That there must be such a power in a society is obvious; for if the good will necessarily recognises rights, the actual will of the members of a society does not. Now the moral end, and freedom to fulfil that end, being absolutely imperative, and all rights being the absolutely necessary conditions of the attainment of freedom and the fulfilment of that moral end, it follows that the rights necessary for the free action of a good will directed to the moral end must be secured even at the cost of coercion of the actual will. Here we reach the paradox, the unavoidable paradox, of state-action. It uses force to create freedom. In order to face this paradox we have to inquire, in the first place what is the body that uses force, and in the second place how far its action is endorsed by the living and active will of the members of the society.

The sovereign authority which uses force must in the ultimate analysis be reduced to the society itself, or rather to the common consciousness of a common end which constitutes the society. If that consciousness creates rights, it creates the sovereignty which is the condition of their maintenance. If, therefore, we give the name of general will to this common consciousness of a common end, expressed in a common will directed to the realisation of that end, we may say that the " general will " is sovereign. Ultimately this is true; but a more realistic analysis, which faces the facts of political life more closely, will reduce the term sovereign to a narrower dimension. It

will assign the term sovereign to " the determinate human superior in receipt of habitual
obedience " of whom Austin spoke, but it
will do so upon condition that behind that
superior, determining his will and inspiring
his acts, is recognised the general will whose
agent he is, and whose purposes he exists to
discover and to realise. This must not be
confused with the assertion that the ultimate
sovereign, *de jure* or *de facto,* is the people. It
is rather an assertion that the ultimate moving
force which inspires and controls political
action is a spiritual force—a common conviction that makes for righteousness, a common
conscience that alone can arm the ministers
and agents of the community with power.
That conviction or conscience at once creates
rights, creates the law or system of rules by
which those rights are maintained, and creates
the sovereign whose mission it is to enunciate
and enforce that law, and to sustain in full
vigour and in complete harmony with one
another all the living institutions which are
the concrete embodiment of rights and of
law.

A common will may thus be expressed in the
whole life of the State, but how shall we
conceive the relation of the individual will to
this common will? Or rather (for the antithesis between the individual and the social
will is abstract and false, since the social will
can only be the will of individuals), can we
believe the reality and conscious presence of
the common will in all, or even in many of the
members of the State? It would at any rate
seem absurd to speak of its conscious presence

in " an untaught and underfed denizen of a
London yard with gin shops on the right hand
and on the left." Green faces the difficulty
with sobriety and caution. After all, he
urges, the moral obligations which we all
acknowledge spring from the same source from
which political subjection arises ; and so far as
we have a lively conscience of the one, so far are
we assenting to the other. In any case we all
of us do, habitually and spontaneously, recognise others and claim recognition for ourselves
as possessors of rights in our ordinary relations
of wage-payers and wage-earners, buyers and
sellers ; and this implies, however unconscious
we may be of the implication, " the needful
elementary conception of a common good
maintained by law." It is true that this makes
us no more than " loyal subjects " ; it is true that
to rise to the height of " intelligent patriotism," a man must have a share in the work
of the State, and must act as a member, or at
any rate vote for the members, of national or
provincial assemblies. But Green does not
enter into the problems of democracy or of
political reform in his Lectures. As we have
seen, he is content to analyse and elucidate the
presuppositions implicit in the actual life of
existing states ; he is content to show that the
fundamental premiss of democracy, that " will,
not force, is the basis of the State," always
is and must be present in every State. He is
unwilling to make a truth which is universal
co-extensive with any particular machinery ;
nor would he imperil such a truth by any over-
emphasis of a particular application. We know
from his actual career, and we may gather from

the logic of his own principles, that he believed in representative government and a wide franchise. But it is what the State can do and should do with its powers that interests him more than its machinery; it is the social problems of the land and of drink that engage his attention most.

But before we turn to these problems, we have to notice another problem in the relation of the individual to the community. We have not only to consider whether by any actual or conscious will the individual endorses the action of the State; we have also to inquire whether, if at all, he can refuse to accept its ruling. The problem of resistance is one bound to arise in a democratic community where the people may readily claim to disobey the law which the people has made: it is particularly apt to arise under a party system, when one party feels strongly that a law or act of government is merely the law or act of an opposite party, and is only based on a temporary majority which has perhaps been gained on some other issue. Green's treatment of the question is sober and cautious, and reminds one in some ways of the treatment of the same question in Plato's *Apology* and *Crito*. The problem is one of conflict between loyalty to natural rights and obedience to the rule of law. The conception of natural rights depends upon the fact that the actual and legal scheme of rights recognised by a given community at a given time is not necessarily perfect. There are other rights—other conditions necessary for the free development of a capacity actually existing in individuals or groups—which in actual law are not recognised, but which nevertheless it is to the common benefit to recognise, since the capacity in question is a capacity for doing something for the common good. To distinguish such rights from legal rights proper we may give them, as we have seen, the name of natural rights, provided that we do not mean thereby that they are the rights of primitive and solitary individuals, but only that they are innate in the constitution of men when living in a society of other men, and are the " natural " or proper conditions of life in such a society. These natural rights may be recognised by the general social conscience of such a society, and yet not be recognised by its laws : they may, indeed, only be recognised by those, perhaps the merest minority, who claim their possession. How far do they warrant resistance to the actual law of the community which embodies the rights it has actually recognised ? How far, for instance, could a sympathiser with the cause of the negro slave resist the master's legal right of property over the slave in the name of the natural right of the slave to be a free man ? In order to give an answer to this question we must distinguish between a natural right already implicitly acknowledged by social conscience, and a natural right not thus acknowledged; and we may concede to the former what we can hardly concede to the latter. The reason for the distinction is plain. The natural right is indeed a necessary condition of a full general welfare, which can only be attained through the liberation of the capacity of every possible contributor; but the whole system of rights

already legally acknowledged is also such a
condition, or rather it is a whole set of such
conditions. Here we see the need for obedience to the rule of law. We must not sacrifice
what is almost the whole for the sake of a part;
we must not risk social chaos, and the disturbance of the existing system of rights, for the
sake of adding a new element to the system.
But when there is already an implicit social
acknowledgment of the claim to a natural
right, we know that there is no possibility of
such sacrifice or such risk. The same force of
a common social consciousness, which is the
ultimate sustainer of legal rights, is here
resisting legal rights for the sake of their
greater perfection. When, however, there is no
implicit acknowledgment of the claim to a
natural right, resistance in the name of such a
right loses its moral justification, and a quiet
propaganda for the creation of such acknowledgment becomes the first step which must be
taken before any resistance can be justifiable.
But even when every condition is satisfied, it
only follows that resistance is possibly justifiable; it does not follow that it is obligatory.

We have not only to conceive of the
State in relation to individuals, but also in
relation to groups, whether the lesser groups
of family or profession which it contains, or
the larger group, the " universal brotherhood,"
in which we may regard it as contained. That
the State is " a society of societies " Green
clearly recognises; and his phrase shows a
grasp of the conception which Gierke, in his
explanation of the " federal " theory of
Althusius and in his own treatise on the

law of corporations, has emphasised. Not only so, but Green recognises that these contained societies—societies presupposed, and not created by the State—have their own inner system of rights, which arises out of their nature as societies. There is a system of rights and duties, for instance, which membership of a family, as such and in itself, entails. The right exercised by the State over the family, and over all similar societies, is a right of adjustment. The State adjusts for each its system of rights internally; and it adjusts each system of rights to the rest externally. Such adjustment has two implications. On the one hand, the rights so adjusted are henceforth held by the individual from the State, and enjoyed by him as a citizen of the State, just because they have been adjusted by the State, and because they are guaranteed in the form to which they have been adjusted. On the other hand, the State which made the adjustments has a certain finality in virtue of its power. Because it is the source of these adjustments, it must be the ultimate power : if it were not so, and if it were itself adjusted, it would not be such a source. But such finality, or if we like such sovereignty, must not be construed as irresponsibility. The State must not be conceived *in vacuo,* or as an almighty Leviathan dwelling in solitude. It stands in relation to other states, and it must adjust itself to those relations in the light of the conception of a " universal brotherhood." Here we touch one of the most distinctive of Green's conceptions—a conception which formed the theoretical justification of an attitude towards war that was already instinctive in his mind.

In establishing the conception of a universal brotherhood, Green starts from the right to life. That right was originally recognised by the members of each particular society as inherent in one another, and in one another only. The stranger was outside the pale, and his life might be taken without breach of right. Gradually the influence of Roman law and of Christianity has led to the universal admission and recognition of the right to life as inherent in all men, simply in virtue of the fact that they are men. Such a universally recognised right implies, as its correlative and guarantor, a universal society. Yet while we thus admit, at any rate implicitly, the right of all men to life, we take it for granted that the exigencies of the State in war neutralise the right; and while an admission of such a right logically implies the idea of one society of mankind, we are apt to suppose that in international dealings that idea can have no place. Green insists on consistency. The right to life was violated, and wrong was done, when an Austrian soldier was shot down by an Italian fighting in the name of a free and united Italy. Nor does it make the wrong right, that such killing should be the only way of attaining the ideal object of a free and united Italy. The disunion of Italy, which only war could end, is not an ultimate fact, such as alone could give an absolute justification to war. That disunion is itself the result of wrong-doing in the past; and the most we are entitled to say of the Italian soldier is that he was only doing wrong, as he did when he killed his Austrian enemy, in order to cure another wrong. War can never be absolutely right: it can only be relatively right, in the sense that it is a " cruel necessity " which has to be faced for the sake of undoing something wrong in the condition of the States engaged in war. War is not an essential attribute of the State as such, in its proper condition; it is rather the attribute of a particular state, in its imperfect actuality. It may be relatively right, in the sense of being a wrong which has to be done in order to right a wrong; but the wrong that is righted—the disunion of Italy, for instance—still remains wrong; and those who committed that ancient wrong are in their dusty graves responsible for the new wrong which puts it right. There is guilt somewhere; there cannot but be guilt somewhere. And just as the ideal object which may involve a war does not condone the guilt, so neither do the moral virtues which war may call into play. War may elicit patriotism; but till the field of peaceful patriotism in the conquest of nature for the service of man and the liberation of man's capacities has been utterly exhausted, there is no need of any resort to war. And Green dreamed, sober and practical as he was, of the ending not only of the need, but even of the impulse. If war is the attribute of the imperfect State, then it follows that the less imperfect States become, the less wars are likely to arise. The better

organised each State, the freer must be the
intercourse of its members with those of other
States; the freer that intercourse, the greater
must be the sense of common interests; the
greater this sense, the more real must be the
common society which it implies.   And thus
" the dream of an international court with
authority resting on the consent of independent States may come to be realised."
All this argument, which constitutes one of
the finest and strongest parts of his Lectures,
illustrates Green's departure from Hegel (who
could hold that " the state of war shows the
omnipotence of the State in its individuality ")
and proves his fellowship with the spirit of
Bright.   He at any rate was far removed from
any conception of the omnipotence or irresponsibility of the State.

But the supreme limitation on the State
lies in its own essence.   Its function is essentially, Green conceives, a negative function.
It is limited to the removal of obstructions
that lie before human capacity as it seeks to
do " things worth doing."   The State has
no positive moral function of making its
members better : it has the negative moral
function of removing the obstacles which prevent them from making themselves better.
The foundation of this view rests on Green's
conception of the nature of moral goodness
in the individual, and of the nature of the
means and methods of action which the
State can employ.   In his view of the nature
of both Green is greatly influenced by Kant.
His conception of the nature of goodness in
the individual is determined by the Kantian

principle of the free will willing itself, and by the correlative principle that a good act is only good when it is done "from a sense of duty" in the doer, and not when it is in its own external character dutiful. Action freely self-determined, in the sense of being determined by the free will acting under a sense of a duty owed by oneself to oneself, is the only moral action. To the inwardness of such a will all State action must in its nature be external. State action cannot ensure the doing of acts from a sense of duty : it can only ensure dutiful acts. What is more, it limits the area of acts done from a sense of duty if it seeks to ensure dutiful acts. What the State must therefore do, in order to leave intact, and even to increase, the area of moral action, is not to seek to enter into the inwardness of the free will, but to ease, as it were, the channels for its issue outwards into action. In Green's phrase, " the effectual action of the State . . . seems necessarily to be confined to the removal of obstacles"; or again, "the function of government is to maintain conditions of life in which morality shall be possible, and morality consists in the disinterested performance of self-imposed duties." Such conditions of life, as we saw before, are rights; and therefore we may say that the function of the State is to enforce the rights, and not to enforce (simply because it cannot, and because, by trying to do so, *pro tanto* it destroys) the righteousness of its members.

This view may seem negative. In truth it is positive enough. In the first place, ir

order to maintain conditions and remove
obstacles, the State must positively interfere
with everything tending to violate conditions
or impose obstacles. It must use force to
repel a force opposed to freedom. In the
second place, its ultimate purpose is always
positive. Liberation of human capacity for
self-determination towards a common good
is that purpose; and nothing can be more
positive. A consideration of punishment may
elicit both points, and illustrate the whole
theory of State interference. Punishment is
not inflicted with any direct reference to the
moral guilt of the offender in the past, or to
his moral reformation in the future. If it
were imposed with reference to moral guilt,
it would have to be graded according to
degrees of moral guilt; and here we are at
once met by the insuperable difficulty, that
moral guilt cannot be measured by degrees,
because we cannot enter into the recesses of
the will to discover its intensity or quality.
If again punishment were imposed with reference to moral reformation in the future, it
would not only lose its power as a deterrent,
but it would deprive the criminal of the
possibility—let us rather say the fundamental duty—of regenerating his own will.
Actually, punishment is adjusted to maintaining the *external* conditions necessary for
the free action of will : it is not adjusted to
the *inner* will itself. It is a force used to
prevent a force opposed to freedom. As such,
its force has to be proportionate to the opposing force. In other words the standard and
measure of punishment is the extent to which

the act punished is a violation, and threatens to produce further violations, of the external conditions necessary for free moral action. (It is always, of course, supposed that such violation is intentional, and that it is only a menace to freedom when it is intentional, and so far as it is intentional. But the degree of intention in the commission of an act is different from the degree of moral guilt in such commission.)

Such a theory does not demoralise punishment, or make it merely negative. Punishment, like all State action, has a moral purpose and a positive quality. It is moral in the sense that its ultimate aim is to secure freedom of action for the moral will of every member of the community. Again it is moral in the sense that the shock and jar of punishment—the interruption it entails in a course of wrong action probably unconsidered—must incidentally induce, or tend to induce (though it may actually fail to do so), some consideration of the meaning of his action in the mind of the criminal punished; some attempt at the regeneration of the will; and, through both some liberation of capacity for self-determination towards a common good. Indeed punishment cannot in any full sense attain its own proper purpose, which is the reassertion of the validity of rights, unless it produces some consciousness of that validity in the offender; and that consciousness to be effective must be due not to the mere feeling that there is external force behind the rights, but to the further feeling that there is some higher and more internal sanction.

In this way we may see that punishment has indirect as well as direct effects. Directly, it is a force preventive of a force opposed to rights—a force whose quantity must be adjusted to the quantity of that other force (as measured by the destruction of rights which it produces), and whose purpose must be its annihilation and, through its annihilation, the restoration of the whole scheme of rights opposed. Indirectly punishment is, and in order to be effectually preventive must be, a reformation of the will, or rather (for the will can only be reformed from within) a shock which makes possible the criminal's reformation of his own will. Even in this latter aspect punishment is still a " removal of obstacles "; for the obstacle which the criminal opposes is not only a force, but a will.

As has already been said, it was social questions which interested Green most. Two of these—the question of education and the question of temperance—his own experience of life had brought home to him very closely; and to these may be added a third in which he was also especially concerned—the problem of property in land. It may seem at first sight a contradiction of his negative formula, that on all three issues Green is in favour of what appears to be a considerable degree of state-intervention. That there is really no such contradiction his lecture at Leicester in 1881, on *Liberal Legislation and Freedom of Contract*, amply shows. Apart from any loftier arguments, the answer may be put on one simple ground. " We must take men as we find them "; and if we find them stumbling over obstacles of ignorance, or drink, or pauperism, we must intervene to remove the ignorance, the drink and the pauperism. We must not postulate, like Herbert Spencer in *The Man versus the State*, an enlightened business man, calmly calculating in his office what are the purposes to which the State must limit its action in a hypothetical prospectus if he is to become a shareholder, and forgetting in the process not only what this immemorial State has done for the countless generations of the past, but also what its infinite activities do for the countless business dealings of to-day. We must rather postulate a landless proletariate, with the ingrained habits of ages of serfdom : overworked women, ill-housed and untaught families : " gin-shops on the right hand and the left." If we start from this basis—and it is the only basis from which a social conscience can start—it is plain that there is much " removal of obstacles " to be done, which cannot be stopped by any plea either of natural rights, or vested rights, or any other rights, or again by any doctrine, however honestly propounded, of the need of leaving scope for free will to ride triumphant of itself over illiteracy, intemperance and indigence. This latter doctrine must in particular be strenuously repudiated. An uncritical idealism too readily runs into the error of claiming everything for free will, as if free will were something independent of and superior to external conditions, and no adjustment of such conditions were necessary for its freedom. The external conditions of life are not external in the sense that they stand outside a consciousness which is independent of them. They are in the consciousness, and they have no existence for man except in so far as they are in his consciousness. If they are in his consciousness, they are part of the self, and self-determination means determination by a self of which they are part. Self-consciousness cannot exist apart from its content; and if the content include " external " things that are evil, the determining self will determine itself accordingly. Any critical idealism must admit the vital importance of " external " things; and a political theory based upon it must recognise that if the State has any duty, it has the duty of so adjusting external conditions, that the self into whose self-determination they enter shall not necessarily determine itself by evil to evil.

The State is entitled on grounds such as these to make education compulsory. The father, on his side, has no " vested " right to leave his son in ignorance; the son, on his side, has a capacity for " doing things worth doing "—worth doing for him, and worth doing for the community—which the community, for his sake and its own sake, has the right to liberate by removing the ignorance that hinders the action of his capacity. There is a right to knowledge in the son, just as much as there is a right to life and liberty, and just for the same reason—that there is a capacity for freely fulfilling a social function to the advantage of the community. We should be inconsistent if we gave the one

right and not the other : and the State has
the " right " to give and to guarantee both,
because the State has always a " right " to
give and to guarantee to each subject, against
all other subjects, anything that is his right.
As with ignorance, so with intemperance. If
the gin-shop is an " external " thing that is
evil, and if intemperance is as much a " hindrance " and an " obstacle " as ignorance,
the State may ask its citizens " to limit, or
even altogether to give up, the not very
precious liberty of buying and selling alcohol,
in order that they may become more free to
exercise the faculties and improve the talents
which God has given them." It makes no
difference that in the one case the State puts
compulsion on the father for the sake of the
son, and in the other it puts compulsion on
each and all for the sake of each and all.   The
one legitimate challenge to Green's position
would lie in urging that the liberty of buying
and selling alcohol does not necessarily constitute a hindrance, as ignorance necessarily
does; or in contending that prohibition is
not *in pári materia* with compulsory education, because prohibition interferes with temperance as well as with intemperance, while
compulsory education only interferes with
absolute ignorance.

We turn to property. Its basis is necessarily the basis of all other rights.   Property
is a condition necessary for the free play of a
capacity which can be exerted for the common
benefit : it is " the means of realising a will,
which in possibility is a will directed to social
good." Thus the fundamental right to life

and liberty postulates as its corollaries on
the one hand, as we have seen, the right of
knowledge, and on the other hand, as we
now see, the right of property. As Aristotle
said, property is " a sum of instruments "
necessary and useful to the individual for pro-
moting the best life of the community. Such
a principle may seem vague. To some it may
seem to justify all private property, as a
necessary ordinance of society : to others it
may seem to condemn private property, since
property, as it now exists in the hands of
capitalists, tends to be used without any regard
to the claims of social obligation. Green runs
to neither of these extremes. On the one hand,
he concedes much to the claims of private
property. He urges that if property is a
means of realising a will *potentially* directed
to social good, it is necessary, not that this
means should always and actually be used
for the social good (an impossible ideal, which
would involve an impossibly inquisitorial
State), but that it should always be able so
to be used. On this ground he defends
property in capital. There is nothing in its
essence which is anti-social. On the contrary, it is constantly being distributed through
the community in wages to labourers and in
profits to those who are engaged in exchange;
nor is there anything in the fact that labourers
are hired in masses by capitalists to prevent
them from being on a small scale capitalists
themselves. On the same ground of potential
social value Green also defends inequality of
property. The social good requires that
different men should fill different positions in

the social whole. Different positions require
different means; and in this way differences
of property are potentially (though they may
not be actually) for the good of society, and
for this reason they may properly be recognised by the social conscience. Moreover,
apart from such direct consideration of social
function, it requires a strong argument to
countervail the presumption in favour of freedom for the individual to acquire and possess,
in whatever measure, the means of realising a
will potentially for the social good. It is only
by the free action of individual wills that the
social good is attained; and inequality of
property may be regarded as the necessary
price for that free action. On the other hand,
we have to remember that some amount of
freedom is needed for every will in the community. Now the need of some freedom for
every will is a presumption against leaving
absolute freedom to a few wills, if we run the
risk of finding the freedom of the many defeated by that of the few. If the free will
requires private property as a means of its
realisation, all free wills require private property; and the system of private property
must be such that all wills can find, and
as far as possible do find, such means. Thus
any kind of property which realises the will
of one man, at the expense of stopping the
realisation of the will of many, is instantly
condemned.

Now it is certain that under our system
of property many men, who possess only a
power of labour and the right to sell it to a
capitalist for bare daily bread, " might as

well, in respect of the ethical purposes which the possession of property should serve, be denied rights of property altogether." Where shall we lay the blame for this melancholy result? On the whole system of property? or on one part of that system? It was the latter answer which Green gave. It was in the condition of one part of the system of property that he saw the fount and origin of evil; it was landed property, as it existed in England, of which he disapproved. Such property, he held, is unique. It is unique in that it is limited : " the capital gained by one is not taken from another, but one man cannot acquire more land without others having less." It is unique in that it is the basis on which the whole tower of modern society rests : " from it alone can be derived the materials necessary for any industry : on it men must find house-room; over it they must pass in communicating with each other." Unique in its nature, landed property has been unique in its history. In the first place the original appropriation was in most countries effected by force. Again the method of exploitation, by means of a system of serfdom, has left consequences which are with us to this day. " Landless countrymen, whose ancestors were serfs, are the parents of the proletariate of great towns." Finally, the process of history has thrown land into the hands of a few; and the development of the law, in the form of family settlements, has prevented those few from alienating their land, while it has given them rights of " doing what they would with their own " which have made

land, the basis of the community's life, less
controlled in the interest of the society than
any other commodity. It is thus to the system of landed property that Green seems
inclined to assign the creation of a proletariate, neither holding nor seeking property.
On a wide view of history one cannot but
admit that there is much truth in the indictment, though one may plead in extenuation
both the good that great landlords have in
many ways done in the past, and the evil
which many capitalists, only too true to the
bad traditions of the old agrarian system,
are in various ways doing to-day. Nor need
we quarrel with Green's practical proposals
for the amelioration of that system as extreme.
He is opposed to family settlements, inimical
as they are both to the freedom of the owner
and to the interest of the community, which
demands, " as a mainstay of social order and
contentment, a class of small proprietors tilling
their own land." He would have the community assert the control it has hitherto failed
to exert over the exercise of the rights of
private property in land; and he would urge
that such control must be close, since the thing
controlled is so absolutely unique. On the
other hand he objects to the appropriation of
" unearned increment " by the State, on the
ground that it could scarcely be attempted
without grave detriment to individual initiative, which might otherwise be directed to the
improvement of the land, and thereby to the
service of society.

Over thirty years have passed since Green
wrote, and to-day a radical idealist might

censure as mere conservatism both some of his
social analysis, as for instance his treatment
of capital, and some of his suggestions of
social policy, as for instance his advocacy of a
class of small proprietors and his deprecation
of any attempt to appropriate unearned increment. But what matters is rather his principles than his analysis of a particular set
of conditions or his suggestions of a particular
policy. If his principles are true, each age
can progressively interpret their meaning to
suit its own needs. Of his general principles
we may at any rate say one thing. He
has seized the philosophy of Greece and of
Germany, and interpreted it for Englishmen
with a full measure of English caution, and
with a full reference to that deep sense of
the "liberty of the subject" and that deep
distrust of "reason of state," which marks
all Englishmen. Partly to this, and partly to
the influence of Kant, we may ascribe his firm
hold on the worth of the individual. He sees
the individual, indeed, not as an unrelated and
therefore unreal atom, but as a member of
society; and he sees that the free will of the
individual must be used not in willing any
and every object, or in willing objects unrelated to the objects of others, but in willing
ideal objects which, as such, are common to
itself and all other wills. But the individual
nevertheless remains the basis of all his thought.
Green is not trammelled by any idealisation of
the majesty of the State; he is more of an
Aristotelian than a Platonist, and more of a
Kantian than a Hegelian. He feels that a
true political theory must recognise the essen-

tial limits imposed upon the State, in all its
dealings with the will of the individual, by its
own nature as a vehicle of force. He feels
that a true theory must also recognise the limits
imposed on the State by the conception of
a universal brotherhood. The State is limited
within; it is also limited without. On the
internal limit Green laid particular emphasis.
" The value of the institutions of civil life lies
in their operation as giving reality to the
capacities of will and reason in the characters
of persons." " The life of the nation has no
real existence except as the life of the individuals composing the nation." The one
standard of national welfare is " worth of
persons." Mill would have endorsed these
words : indeed he himself wrote words which
were practically identical. On this basis of
" the worth of persons " Green, like Mill,
erected a distinction, which might serve to
limit the power of the State and to defend the
freedom of the individual, between acts which
the State can control and acts which it cannot
touch. There is a great difference, however,
between the distinction made by Mill and that
made by Green. Mill makes a false distinction
between self-regarding and other-regarding
actions. Green makes a true distinction between outward actions necessary and valuable
for the maintenance of rights—actions which
the State can secure by external force because
they are external—and actions proceeding
from an inward will, which are only valuable
when they proceed from such a will and which
therefore cannot be secured by any external
force. The one type of action not only may

but ought to be enforced, because such enforcement is necessary to worth of persons : the other type of action not only cannot but ought not to be enforced, because enforcement is detrimental to such worth. And yet we must remember, even while we emphasise the limits imposed on the State by this distinction, that the State has a final moral value, and *is* majestical, even in its limits and even because of its limits. If it does not interfere with morality, it is for the sake of morality that it refrains : if it does interfere with external acts, it is also for the sake of morality that it intervenes. It is a moral being, animated by a moral purpose. If we do not take our morality from it, from it we take the rights which are the conditions of morality, and through it therefore we are moral. The State is the source and giver of our rights. Rights may have existed in the family before they existed in the State; when the State has come and guaranteed those rights, they exist in the State and proceed from the State. Ideal rights may be conceived which are not in the State : only when they are in it do they become real rights. We may be right to challenge the State in the name of ideal rights : we should have no conception of any rights without the State. If we challenge the State, we must challenge it in fear and trembling. The presumption is always against us. The whole system of acknowledged rights is almost certain to claim, and to deserve, a higher allegiance than the most ideal of ideal rights.

CHAPTER III

THE IDEALIST SCHOOL—BRADLEY AND BOSANQUET

A PRESENTATION of the State more Hegelian than that attempted by Green appears in the chapter of Mr. Bradley's *Ethical Studies* entitled " My Station and its Duties." Briefly, and perhaps for that reason erroneously, it may be said that this chapter combines the Platonic conception of " justice " with the Hegelian conception of *Sittlichkeit.* Plato had conceived justice (or more properly righteousness—the fulfilment of the whole duty of man) to be attained in a community, and in its members, when each member took his post or station in the community, and discharged faithfully and solely the function of that post or station. Hegel, again, had conceived of a social righteousness—there is no English word for *Sittlichkeit*—which was neither the subjective morality of an inward conscience nor the external legality of mere law, but blended and transcended both. Social righteousness is a spirit and habit of life expressed in the social opinion and enforced by the social conscience of a free people; it is at one and the same time a mind or self-consciousness, because it is a spirit, and a thing or external existence, because it is a visible system of habit and conduct. By it our relations to one another are controlled; and since our relations flow from our position or station in the community —or rather, since the sum of the relations in which we stand constitutes our position or station—we may say that it controls our position or station. Social righteousness is in us, and we are righteous in a fuller sense than we can be under " morality " or under law, when we fulfil our station among our people in the sense that it demands. Then the spirit of our people dwells in us, and " our life is hid with our fellows in the common life of our people."

Both Plato and Hegel thus imply the idea of a moral organism. If, as Plato says, there is a function appropriate to my position which it is righteousness for me to discharge, then, in order to explain my function, I must pre-suppose an organic moral whole or system —organic, in the sense of determining the functions of its parts towards the fulfilment of its own final end, and moral, in the sense that its final end is moral, and its parts are moral agents. If, again, as Hegel says, " the spirit of a nation (which is a spirit of social righteous-ness) controls and entirely dominates from within each person," so that " he feels it to be his own very being " and " looks upon it as his absolute final aim," then we must postu-late an " organic actuality " of a moral order to explain that spirit. It is this conception of a moral organism which Bradley urges. It is implied in daily experience, and it is the only explanation of that experience. " In fact, what we call an individual man is what he is because of and by virtue of community, and communities are not mere names, but some-thing real." Already at birth the child is what he is in virtue of communities : he has something of the family character, something

of the national character, something of the
civilised character which comes from human
society. As he grows, the community in
which he lives pours itself into his being in
the language he learns and the social atmosphere he breathes, so that the content of his
being implies in its every fibre relations of
community. He is what he is by including
in his essence the relations of the social State;
and if morality consists in the fulfilment of
self, it consists in the fulfilment of those relations. But those relations constitute his
position or station; and therefore we may
say that his morality consists in the fulfilment
of his station and its duties. If we leave out
of sight for the present the question, whether
the self is exhausted in the relations of the
social State, or also contains still higher
relations in a " Kingdom of Heaven," we may
say that " a man's life with its moral duties is
in the main filled up by his station in that
system of wholes which the State is, and that
this partly by its laws and institutions, and
still more by its spirit, gives him the life which
he does live and ought to live." And regarding the State as a system, in which many
spheres (the family, for instance) are subordinated to one sphere, and all the particular
actions of individuals are subordinated to
their various spheres, we may call it a moral
organism, a systematic whole informed by a
common purpose or function. As such it has
an outer side—a body of institutions; it has
an inner side—a soul or spirit which sustains
that body. And since it is a moral organism—
since, that is to say, its parts are themselves

conscious moral agents—that spirit resides in those parts and lives in their consciousness. In such an organism—and this is where it differs from an animal organism, and why we have to use the word moral—the parts are conscious : they know themselves in their position as parts of a whole, and they therefore know the whole of which they are parts. So far as they have such knowledge, and a will based upon it, so far is the moral organism self-conscious and self-willing; and this is what Hegel means by speaking of the State as a " self-conscious " ethical substance, a " self-knowing and self-actualising individual." The will and the knowledge are the will and the knowledge of persons, but of persons (1) who have as the content of their will the moral organism on its outer side, as a body of relations, and (2) who are aware of themselves as willing this content, and thereby constitute the moral organism on its inner side as the spirit of a nation.

Thus, on the one hand, we must recognise that the State lives; that there is a nation's soul, self-conscious in its citizens; and that to each citizen this living soul assigns his field of accomplishment. Yet on the other hand we must recognise that individuals live, and live with all their fulness just when and just so much as they cultivate their specific field. " The breadth of my life is not measured by the multitude of my pursuits, nor the space I take up amongst other men; but by the fulness of the whole life which I know as mine." This may seem a facile reconciliation of the free moral will with the system of the State,

achieved at the cost of the suppression of one
of the factors and the impossible exaltation
of the other. And Mr. Bradley himself, while
arguing that fulfilment of station is a good
enough practical canon of morality, does not
argue that it is a perfect or complete ideal.

It does not, indeed, affect the validity of
such a canon of morality to contend that
the whole scheme of the State, and the
functions which it assigned, were in times
past such as our moral will cannot to-day
recognise. That contention can be met by
the reply that if we admit any evolution of
man towards an end, evolution involves stages
of growth; and in each stage the essence of
man is realised, as far as that stage of his
growth permits, by the scheme of the State,
which can therefore demand recognition from
his moral will. But there are other con-
tentions which are more vital, and these
Mr. Bradley himself urges. The State of to-
day may not be reconcilable with the morality
of to-day. The State may be in a confused or
decadent condition; short of that, it may,
being as it is in a state of development, retain
unresolved elements of its past, which are
opposed to ideal morality. Again, we have to
reckon with cosmopolitan morality in the individual, who may seek to transcend the
function allotted to his station in a particular
community; we must recognise, for instance,
the desire to produce philosophic truth or
artistic beauty of a universal value, which can
hardly be connected with the duty of a station.
Such recognition may serve to drive us, or to
lift us, to the conception of a higher organism

E

than that of the State. By faith we may come
to believe in the realisation of a society of all
humanity as a divine organic whole; or, as
St. Paul wrote, we may come to see that we
are organs, diversely endowed, " unto the
building up of the body of Christ," which is
" fitly framed and knit together through that
which every joint supplieth."

If we venture on any criticism of the doctrine of " my station and its duties," it would
take the following direction. The full Hegelian
doctrine of the State is a doctrine of more
than the State, and for that reason it cannot
be accepted as a doctrine of the State. Hegel's
State is really society as well as the State. It
is the whole complex of influences arising from
the fact of association. Such a synthesis is
the result of that " German instinct for comprehension," which, as Green says in his
lectures on *The English Commonwealth*, " has
no difficulty in regarding Church and State as
two sides of the same spiritual organism."
But just as we must distinguish Church
and State, so we must distinguish State and
society. Failure to distinguish Church and
State merges the Church in the State, and
produces the mere territorial Church as an
appendage of the territorial State; and failure
to distinguish State and society may lead to
unlimited State regulation of life. It is safer
to distinguish, as we in England have always
distinguished, between society (with its
" social " atmosphere, its " social " morality,
and its " social " institutions) and the State
(with its political institutions, its laws, and its
officials). Both are sustained by the same

moral purpose : they overlap, they blend, they borrow from one another. But roughly we may say that the area of the one is voluntary co-operation, its energy that of good will, its method that of elasticity : while the area of the other is rather that of mechanical action, its energy force, its method rigidity. If we draw such a distinction—if we thus conceive the State as regulating externals by force (though always with the ultimate aim of righteousness), then we necessarily adopt a more cautious attitude to the State. It will not be a merely negative attitude, or a defence of the " individual " against the State, as if the State were in its nature something hostile. Our attitude will be rather one of reluctance to fly to the *ultima ratio* of political mechanism until we are sure that we have exhausted social resources and found them inadequate, or again, until we have tried and tested some elastic social method, and found it answer so well and so unfailingly that it may safely be made into a binding and rigid rule enforced by the State. For far from defending man *versus* the State, we shall not even defend society *versus* the State, if the State can attain better than society the aims which are common to them both.[1]

---

[1] Hegel distinguishes between State and society (more properly " civil society "), but in a different sense. " Society " is for him the economic organisation, with its system of wants, its production to meet those wants, and its division of labour (resulting in differentiation of classes) to carry on that production. It is the same body of men as constitutes the State, but at a lower power, and in a lower aspect. The State, or political organisation, takes it up and transforms it into something higher.

Drawing this distinction, we can endorse, from our different point of view, much of Hegel's philosophy. State and society, taken together as one, do constitute such an objective and outward scheme of goodness as may form the content of our will. When we try to fill our place in that scheme, we may find that our station and its duties completely satisfy the demands of our moral nature. In Green's phrase, we may say (1) that through the State the moral ideal receives " increasing concreteness in a complex organisation of life, with laws and institutions, with relationships, courtesies and charities, with arts and graces "; and (2) that through the State, " through inheritance and education," through the operation of social institutions and arts, we receive a " corresponding discipline," which enables us to pursue that ideal. Yet in saying this, we must remember, with Green, the other side of the matter. We must remember (1) that the State proper, the State as such, can only promote morality indirectly, by the removal of obstacles, or, in other words, by the guarantee of rights, which are not morality but the conditions of morality. If we forget this limitation of the State, we are in danger of so idealising the State that we surrender the whole of life to its regulation. We must remember (2) that whatever society and the State may give to our morality, we have to make what they give utterly and entirely our own, before it is moral. The motive must be our motive, the object our object, the whole will must be the free utterance of ourselves. Of this truth, so strongly enunciated by Kant,

Hegel is indeed perfectly well aware. What he seeks to do is, as it were, to *fill* this free will, which in itself is bare and ignorant of any object, with the content of the social system. He would transcend the mere " morality " of such a bare will by the " social righteousness " of a will equally free but far richer in content. The difficulty is to see how the free will can always find full and free satisfaction in apprehending and taking its place in the system of social righteousness. The will may fail to apprehend the scheme, which in that case remains foreign to itself; or it may apprehend it, but find that it falls short of its own demands, and in that case the scheme still remains foreign. We may comfort ourselves by saying that the one case only presents us with the imperfect man, and the other with the imperfect society. But before we can really take such comfort to ourselves, we must face fully the problem of the imperfect man and the imperfect society. Before we can see in the social system the realisation of the free will, we must consider the man whose will the society transcends, and the man whose will transcends the society.

This is what Bosanquet, in *The Philosophical Theory of the State*, has attempted. Bosanquet adopts Green's principles, but uses the social experience of a later day and the aid of psychological research to carry Green's conclusions further. In the light of a fuller experience and of fresh data he would sweep away some of the limitations with which Green had hedged about his doctrine of the State as the organ for the realisation of free will; and

he would thus bring Green's philosophy **to a**
point where it approaches close to, **if it does**
not altogether blend with, the full **Hegelian**
conception of the State.

In constructing his own theory of the State,
Bosanquet starts by a vindication of Rousseau.
He sets Rousseau in his true place as the
founder (or rather the refounder) of the idealist
or philosophical theory of the State; and he
shows the debt which the German idealists
owed, and acknowledged that they owed, **to**
Rousseau's conception of the liberty of the
individual, of the " general will " of the State,
and of the relation of the two to one another.
The theory which he himself expounds, after
and on the basis of a sympathetic analysis. of
the *Contrat Social*, is in its fundamentals
identical with that of Green. His conception
of the nature and limits of state-action is, like
that of Green, negative. The State, as such,
has force as the instrument, external things
as the area, and the " hindrance of hindrances "
to human capacity as the function, of the action
which it can undertake. This principle, drawn
from Kant, and identical with that adopted by
Green, rests ultimately on the idea of the
supreme and final value of the autonomy of the
good will. The State can secure the conditions
of the freedom of that will by using force to
repel any force, and hindrances to repel any
hindrance, which are hostile to its exercise;
what it cannot do is to direct or control that
will itself. The conditions which the State
secures are rights; and rights are therefore
regarded by Bosanquet, as they are by Green,
as concerned with the external conditions

which are necessary for the free action of the
good will.

Along this line Bosanquet is led to that distinction between the State as such—the State
as a political organisation using force—and
society with all its social institutions, of which
we have already spoken.   By society he under-
stands that vast complex of social co-operation,
which is associated, in various degrees, with
the State and its activities.   It is this field of
social co-operation which supplies the inventive
and experimental element in the life of the
community;   and the work of the State is for
the most part a work of endorsement, in the
sense that it seals with the seal of its force the
approved results of this flexible element.   At
the same time we must not think that such a
statement exhausts or fully explains the relations of State and society.   Society, after all,
is within the State, and it has its meaning in
the State.   It follows that, if we take the State
in its fuller sense, not as a political mechanism
using force, but as a general organisation and
synthesis of life, which includes and correlates
all other organisations, we shall see it as a group
of groups, a community of communities, embracing and sustaining the whole field of social
co-operation.   In this sense we can view the
meaning of the State from two aspects.   We
can see it first of all as a source of adjustments,
criticising and adjusting, in the light of a working conception of life as a whole, the institutions which it contains, and reducing them by
such criticism to an ordered and graded system.
We can see it again as a driving-wheel, giving
motive power to the system—as a " force " in-

vigorating by a constant reminder and suggestion of their duties every member and every
institution, and preventing the lethargy and
inertia into which, without such reminder and
suggestion, they might too readily fall. Nor can
the State act in this second aspect, as a force,
unless it has present to itself its first aspect of
itself as a working conception of life as a whole.
" The State, as such, is limited to the office of
maintaining the external conditions of a good
life; but the conditions cannot be conceived
without reference to the life for which they
exist, and it is true, therefore, to say that the
conception of the Nation-State involves at least
an outline of the life to which, as a power, it
is instrumental."

If we thus regard the State as involving, and
in one of its aspects being, a working conception
of life as a whole, we come nearer to the philosophy of Hegel. And this closer approximation to Hegel marks *The Philosophical Theory
of the State* in various ways. In the first place
Bosanquet abandons Green's cautious and
hesitating treatment of the relation of the free
will of the average citizen to the State and its
institutions, and comes closer to the Hegelian
conception of the free absorption of the individual in the spirit of a nation. This is due in
large measure to a fuller social experience,
the fruit of new social experiments, which
suggests that the essentials of character are
the same throughout the social whole; that
the poor are as alive as the rich (one may
almost say that owing to the trend of recent
legislation, by which they have been so intimately affected, they are more alive than the

rich) to the meaning and importance of the
State; in a word, that a common social consciousness pervades the whole community.
But the change is also due to a change in
the method of inquiry. It owes something to
the growth of psychological inquiry and data.
We have realised through this growth how
much there is in our minds that is subconscious, and how closely that subconscious
element is related with and how easily it passes
into the conscious. We have come to feel that
" there is no abrupt division between our conscious mind and the social system of suggestion,
custom and force "—that " the two are related
much as the focus of consciousness is related
to the subconscious and automatic habits by
which daily life is rendered possible." Yet if
the State is largely a subconscious element in
our mind, it is none the less there; and at any
moment of crisis it comes with a rush to the
forefront of our consciousness.

The psychological method takes Bosanquet
still nearer to Hegel. Hegel treated the State
under the head of objective mind; he spoke
of the State as a self-consciousness, " a
self-knowing and self-actualising individual."
Bosanquet travels the same path in analysing
the nature of institutions. He urges that the
actual reality of any institution " lies in the
fact that certain living minds are connected in
a living way." Parliament, for instance, is
not some six hundred men sitting in a room;
it is fundamentally a connecting idea, which
being concerned with action is a purpose as
well as an idea—a purpose common to six
hundred minds and uniting six hundred minds

C 2

in a common experience. Such an idea backed
by a purpose we may call an ethical idea; and
so we may speak of institutions as ethical ideas,
and we may say that, as such, they are that
common substance of individual minds which
unites them as a single or common mind.
Parliament, in the last resort, is neither bricks
and mortar, nor flesh and blood : it is the
substance common to six hundred minds; it
is, as we say, the " common mind." All the
institutions of a country, so far as they are
effective, are not only products of thought and
creations of mind : they *are* thought, and they
are mind. Otherwise we have a building
without a tenant, and a body without a mind.
An Oxford college is not a group of buildings,
though common speech gives that name to such
a group : it is a group of men. But it is not
a group of men in the sense of a group of bodies
in propinquity : it is a group of men in the
sense of a group of minds. That group of
minds, in virtue of the common substance of
a uniting idea, is itself a group-mind. There
is no group-mind existing apart from the minds
of the members of the group; the group-mind
only exists in the minds of its members. But
nevertheless it exists. There is a college mind,
just as there is a Trade Union mind, or even a
" public mind " of the whole community; and
we are all conscious of such a mind as something
that exists in and along with the separate minds
of the members, and over and above any sum
of those minds created by mere addition.

Thus, we may maintain (1) that institutions
are ethical ideas common to a number of minds,
and have value and life as such. Of course

they must be embodied in outward form—
bricks and mortar, flesh and blood; and, of
course, again they must be accepted, and as it
were collaborated in, by a far wider area of
minds than that of those immediately concerned. The college must be an idea accepted
by parents and the general public, as well as
entertained by its fellows and undergraduates;
parliament must be an idea which electors
accept and in which electors collaborate, as
well as an idea entertained by members of
Parliament. Otherwise the college teaches
and the Parliament legislates in vain; " they
have no hold," as we say, " on public opinion."
And, further, we may maintain (2) that if an
institution is an ethical idea, it postulates a
mind that entertains the idea, and entertains
it not in the sense of knowing it or of having
heard about it, but in the sense of willing it
and working it. Such a mind we may call the
mind of the institution, or the mind of the
group immediately concerned with the institution, though of course we must always remember that just because it is mind it must
exist in the minds of the members of the
institution or group, and cannot exist elsewhere.
But all that has hitherto been said of institution can also be applied to the State itself.
The State is an institution. The State is an
ethical idea; or rather, it is *the* ethical idea,
since it is the final working conception of life
as a whole. As such an idea, it is the common
substance of the minds of all the citizens,
which, so far as they are animated, consciously
or subconsciously, by itself, unites them into
a single mind. And so we come to Hegel's

conception of the State as " the self-conscious
ethical substance "; and we see the State as
the common or universal mind of its members.

In his theory of punishment, and in his
attitude to the problem of the application of
moral standards to State-action, Bosanquet
also appears to depart to some extent from
Green. Recognising with Green that reformation of the criminal must enter, if only second-
arily, into the purpose of punishment, he seems
to differ from Green in assigning to punishment
a peculiarly positive quality, which modifies
the general theory of the negative character of
State-action. The argument he uses is of a
psychological character. Human nature has
a subtle continuity; and what happens in the
subconscious region of automatic action may
produce sympathetic results in the region of
consciousness. If by a careless reflex or automatic action, as, for instance, by riding care-
lessly on a bicycle round the corner, I have an
accident and suffer the shock of pain, my consciousness is affected, and my conscious will
may henceforth be directed to control that area
of action. Similarly if by casual action in the
realm of duties (a realm largely automatic,
because I do most of my duties as a matter of
habit, without reflection) I commit some slip—
forgetting, for instance, to discharge my duties
as trustee—and if, as a result, I suffer the shock
of a legal action, my conscious will may be
awakened, and stimulated to control that area
of action, which the shock brings me to recognise consciously as a matter of obligation. Thus
punishment may mean, not that henceforth I
cease to have slips because I fear to experience

a like shock again, but that henceforth I cease
to have slips because I have come to my senses;
have had my consciousness of the meaning of a
whole system of habits awakened; and have
realised, in the light of such consciousness,
what my offending means. It is possible to
accept this account of the working of the re-
formatory side of punishment, and yet to doubt
whether it differentiates punishment from
other forms of State-action. Perhaps *any*
form of State-compulsion may awaken consciousness of the meaning and necessity of a
range of duty hitherto not apprehended; and
the father, for instance, may have a new sense
of parental responsibility awakened by being
compelled to send his child to school, even
before he is punished, or even without being
punished, for not so doing. Thus all State-
action, and not punishment only, may have a
supervening justification of this nature, and
come to assume the positive quality, which
Bosanquet vindicates for punishment alone.

Where Bosanquet seems to part company
with Green most decidedly is in his treatment
of the morality of State-action. We have seen
how Green condemned war as wrong, because it
violated a right to life and liberty, belonging
to men in virtue of their common humanity,
and therefore postulating a " universal brotherhood " in which all men are joined together
by their common recognition of its validity.
Bosanquet deals with the question in a different
way. He argues, in the first place, that a distinction has to be drawn between the acts of the
State as such, and the personal acts of its statesmen or agents; and he insists on the impro-

priety of applying to acts which belong to the
first sphere the moral terms (murder, theft and
so forth) which belong to the second. In the
next place, and in order to explain this im-
propriety, he urges that the State " cannot, as
a State, act within the relations of private life
in which organised morality exists." The
State is " the guardian of our whole moral
world, and not a factor in our organised moral
world." It cannot be bound by the system of
rights and duties which it makes binding on
its members; it cannot be limited by the
social ethics it maintains. At most, we can
criticise its actions on the ground that they
embody a low conception of the good, or that
they involve means inappropriate to realise a
true conception; but in such criticism we criticise the State not in relation to any wider good
or any more general morality to which it should
conform, but in regard only to its own good
and its own morality. Another view of this
matter, to which some of us would rather cling,
would emphasise far more strongly the responsibility of the State for its agents, and the
responsibility of both the State and its agents
at the bar of civilised opinion. French law
admits the legal responsibility of the State for
those acts of its agents which are acts of administration : and any true theory of the State
surely demands its legal responsibility for the
acts of its organs when they are acting as
organs.[1] If a citizen can thus treat his own

---

[1] The great objection to the Trades Disputes Act of
1906 is that it contravenes the fundamental doctrines
(1) that a group, just because it has a mind and a will,
must be responsible, and (2) that a group, just because,

State as legally responsible for damage, it is difficult to see why a State, which can undergo legal responsibility, should not also undergo moral responsibility, if there is any body of moral opinion to affix responsibility. Such a body of civilised opinion, a system of Social Ethics or *Sittlichkeit*, transcending the limits of the Nation-State, and common to the majority of States in Western Europe and America, does exist. It seems difficult to see why such a body of opinion should not affix moral responsibility for anything which it regards as a breach of its own code; though that, of course, is quite another matter from any attempt to enforce legal responsibility. Surely one may say, that while a State cannot be responsible to its law for its dealings with other States (though it can be so responsible for its dealings with its own citizens), and while again it cannot be responsible for such dealings to a higher system of law, since none such yet exists, yet it can be responsible, and should be responsible, in a moral sense, for all its acts (which include the acts of its organs when they are acting as organs) to the common body of moral opinion in Christendom. Are we not too full of the zeal of the State, if we insist overmuch on the fact that it transcends its own organs, or if again we emphasise unduly the finality and supremacy of the State as the " guardian of a whole moral world " ? Great Britain is the final and supreme arbiter to her citizens of rights and duties : she is the final

as a group, it can only act—for the most part—through organs or agents, must be responsible for the acts of those organs or agents.

giver to them all of the stuff of their social morality—in other words, of their " national character." But even to them she must be responsible for her doings, which are the doings of those who act in her name—even to them, because they are part of that civilised world in which she stands, and by whose opinion she is judged.

In leaving the idealist school, we must take some account of the criticisms which it has to face. First and most obvious is the criticism that it does not deal with things as they are. The State of which it conceives, resting on the free consent and co-operation of the moral will of every citizen, may be laid up in heaven, but it is not established on earth. Such a criticism, however, rests on an entire misconception of the method of political theory. Political theory, like ethical theory, is concerned with what may be called the " pure " instance—with the conscience of the good man, and the " general will " of the right State. It assumes that the best is the truest, and that the truest is the proper subject of study. Politics and ethics are alike concerned with man at his highest power, and not at his lowest; " for the real nature of a thing is what the thing is when its growth is fully developed." There will always be some who will use the lower as the criterion of the higher; there will always be others—and they are not necessarily mistaken— —who will use the higher as the criterion of the lower. In any case the idealist does not stand alone in making the ideal the subject of study. Sidgwick was a Utilitarian; but Sidgwick holds that the study of politics " is concerned primarily with . . . the system of relations which *ought to be* established . . . in a society of civilised men." [1]

Another criticism of the idealist school, which at first sight appears very different, is that of the ardent social reformer. What the idealist does, he urges, is not to construct an ideal, but to idealise the given data of imperfect society, and to preach the divine right of things as they are. By putting an ideal interpretation on the existing institutions of society, he reconciles the social conscience to things which it ought not to accept. Aristotle idealised slavery; Green idealised capital. From this point of view Mr. Hobson, in *The Crisis of Liberalism*, can rank idealism as a part of " the tactics of Conservatism." The same indictment would urge, from another point of view, that the idealist is so concerned with the spiritual foundations of society in the human conscience, so occupied with the inward man and the autonomy of his free will, that he is blind to the need of reform of material conditions. He is obsessed by " the claims of individual moralisation "; he says in his heart, with Aristotle, that evils arise not " out of the possession of private property," but " from the wickedness of human nature "; and basing himself on the prime necessity of the freedom of the moral will, he reduces the State, which ought to cure these evils, to the mere negative

[1] Sidgwick's *Elements of Politics* (1891) has not been discussed in this volume (though the book is one which every student of political theory should know), because, late as is its date, it belongs to the Utilitarian period of Bentham and Mill, which is the subject of another volume in this series.

function of removing obstacles and hindering hindrances. The reader may judge for himself, from what has already been said of the teaching of Green and Bradley and Bosanquet, how far such criticism is just.

Another and prevalent line of criticism is directed against the intellectualism of the idealist school. Idealist thinkers, it is said, ascribe too much to the conscious will and reasoning mind. There *is* a sphere of will and reason; but there are also other spheres. Man is a part of nature, set in the midst of all the play of selection and survival and evolution; and the biologist must have his say in any full political theory. Again, and still more, man is a creature compact of emotions, impulses and instincts, as well as of conscious reason. He has a whole subconscious side of his nature, on which suggestion plays; where associations of ideas are formed; where imitation grows, and habits have their dwelling-place. Here the social psychologist enters to demonstrate the inadequacy of the idealist and his own necessity. Writers like Dr. MacDougall and Mr. Graham Wallas contend that the idealist— and for that matter the utilitarian also—start from premises about the human mind which are altogether too bare and too jejune. They start from a rational faculty armed with a few simple principles of " the common good " or " the greatest happiness of the greatest number "; whereas a full philosophy should start from a full man, armed with " all thoughts, all passions, all delights, whatever fills this mortal frame."

The two succeeding chapters will show, or at any rate attempt to show, how far this last line of criticism is warranted. There is one thing, however, which should be said at once. When the idealist says that the State is the product of reason and the rational will, he does not mean that reason has been consciously and explicitly creating political institutions during the course of history. That would be an impossible contention. He means that a development has taken place, which, when we look at its course and its results, we can explain to our reason as something rational—something which is directed to ends of which reason approves. And he argues, therefore, that human reason has been present all the time, implicit and immanent, groping its way, by experiment on experiment, towards its ends. If it had not been present, the development would have ended not, as it has done, in a rational system of organised life which our reason can understand, but in a confused amalgam of taboos and instincts and habits which would have no meaning, no connection, and no reason. Nor, again, does the idealist contend that all the political action of the ordinary citizen to-day is the result of conscious reason. Such action may in large measure be the result of habit or unconscious imitation. What the idealist means is that the actions of the citizen are rational, in the sense that they admit of a rational explanation. And he contends, not unfairly, that this means that reason is after all present, and is the real dominant force, however much habit or imitation may serve as its ally by helping to produce acts which are the sort of acts that reason would wish to have done.

CHAPTER IV

THE SCIENTIFIC SCHOOL—HERBERT SPENCER

Most of the political writings of **J. S.** Mill appeared after 1848. The Essay on *Liberty*, for instance, was published in 1859, and the Essay on *Representative Government* appeared in 1860. But Mill belongs to an old tradition, though he gave that tradition a deeper and more spiritual interpretation; and he must be regarded as the last of the great Utilitarians, rather than as the first among the new prophets who have arisen since 1848. In Herbert Spencer a new element definitely appears. It is true, as we shall see, that while he attacked what he called the " expediency philosophy " of Bentham, he was always a Utilitarian in his politics. Happiness is the end he proposes, though he insists that it must be happiness willed by the Creator, which issues in the form of free energy of faculty, and not happiness willed by the State, which assumes the form of an enjoyment connected with the possession of wealth; and just as Bentham had held that freedom for each individual to judge and pursue his own interests was the chief condition of material happiness, so Spencer believes that the law of equal freedom for each individual supplies the chief means to the happiness which consists in energy of faculty. But already in *Social Statics*, which was published in 1851, Spencer has begun his distinctive method of interpreting ethics and politics as analogous to, and indeed as part of, the science of the laws of

84

life. " Morality," he already writes, " is essentially one with physical truth—is in fact a species of transcendental physiology." What we have now to consider is thus the interpretation of human life in terms of natural science.

In Spencer this interpretation is confused. He did not really approach politics through science, without preconceptions drawn from other sources, and with the sole idea of eliciting the political lessons which science might teach. On the contrary he was already charged with political preconceptions when he approached science, and he sought to find in science examples or analogies to point a moral already drawn and adorn a tale whose plot was already sketched. The fundamental confusion which he never surmounts is due to the fact that the *a priori* conceptions of individual rights with which he starts do not and cannot accord with the organic and evolutionary conception of the State which he attains through the use of natural science. His philosophy consequently begins and ends as " an incongruous mixture of Natural Rights and physiological metaphor." At first sight this confusion may seem a curious anomaly, so stern and so severe is the logic which apparently pervades his writings. But Spencer's logic is really bare and mechanical. It is a matter of constant antitheses which are too clear-cut to correspond to life, and of constant application of the fallacious argument of the Sorites, which any experience of practical life compels most men to reject. There is none of that rich feeling for reality, and none of that attempt to resolve and transcend antitheses, which marks the logic of Hegel.

To understand the discrepant elements in Spencer's political theory, we are driven to inquire into the sources of his thought. He does not start from any single source; he draws his inspiration from many different sources, which he tries, but fails, to gather together into a single whole. The first source we may notice was English Radicalism. He sprang, as he says, from a family " essentially dissenting " and, as such, opposed to authority; and his Nonconformist instincts, and the Nonconformist training of his youth, left an abiding mark. By his uncle, the Rev. Thomas Spencer, an advanced theologian, who regarded the Church as a growth which needed continual adaptation to external conditions, he was led to take an active interest in Radical politics. Thomas Spencer was associated with Joseph Sturge of Birmingham, who had founded in 1841 a weekly called the *Nonconformist*, and who was one of the leading spirits of the Complete Suffrage Union. It was to the *Nonconformist* that Herbert Spencer contributed in 1842 his first essay on *The Proper Sphere of Government*, and it was as Secretary of the Derby branch of the Complete Suffrage Union that he first took an active part in politics. He joined in an agitation against bribery at elections; and he also took part, rather by writing than by speaking, in the movements against the Corn Laws and the State-Church. This had been his training when, in the course of 1847, he began to compose his first political treatise, to which he gave the name of *Social*

Statics. But after the end of 1848 he was, as
sub-editor of the *Economist*, brought into contact with Thomas Hodgskin; and this contact
probably influenced the development of *Social
Statics* very vitally. Hodgskin was an anti-
Benthamite Radical. Like Godwin he believed in the natural rights of humanity, at
which Bentham had scoffed. He extended to
politics as well as to economics the doctrine of
laissez-faire, whereas Bentham, leaving economics to the free play of natural forces, had
claimed law and politics as the sphere of
scientific regulation. Society, Hodgskin held,
was a natural phenomenon with natural laws
assigned to it by the universal spirit, or supreme moral force, in order that its members
might by their aid create a just order of the
world. The function of government was accordingly negative : it extended only to the
securing of a free field for the operation of
natural laws; and human laws were as pre-
judicial as natural laws were the reverse.
The ultimate goal and Utopia of the future
was thus a state of anarchy, in which government had disappeared, and the sentiments
of each were automatically adjusted in a
spontaneous harmony with those of all.

So far as we have gone, it would appear that
it was in his early Radical environment, and
also, and more particularly, in his contact with
Hodgskin, that Spencer found the primary and
main source of the political creed which he
always championed. In 1850 he had, as he himself tells us, read very little; and all that he
knew of Bentham, when he attacked him, was
the simple fact that he advocated a scientific

application of the principle of the greatest
happiness of the greatest number. But there
were two other sources, somewhat incompatible
both with one another and with his early
Radicalism, on which Spencer also drew. These
were the study of natural science, in which he
had always been interested, and in which his
experience of engineering had interested him
still further; and an inkling of the German
idealism of Schelling and Schlegel, which he had
gained from a cursory reading of Coleridge.
From German idealism he drew what he calls
in *Social Statics* the " idea of life." Life, he
learned to think, is not a fact of nature to be
studied by a positive science, but a transcendental principle, in virtue of which nature as a
whole, and society as a part of nature, evolve
from within outwards towards a final " individuation." Life is the cause of a universal
evolution : in fact it *is* universal evolution—for
Spencer was even willing to include the phenomena of the solar system in the " idea of life."
It follows from what has been said that Spencer
did not start from biology, the positive science
of life in the restricted sense of that word; nor
did he borrow the idea of evolution from biology
in order to extend it to the universe. He
started with the idea of a universal evolution,
in which he afterwards included biological evolution. Already in 1840 Lyell's *Principles* had
suggested to his mind the hypothesis of development; but it was Coleridge, and Schelling
through Coleridge, who gave precise form to
the hypothesis. In all nature, he came to
argue, and therefore in human society,there is a
transcendental and divine force of life. Hence

it follows that nature and society are living organisms : it follows that in virtue of their immanent life they develop; and this development may be regarded as a process of individuation or differentiation, which is combined with co-ordination of the differentiated elements. The higher the individuation, the greater the value; and thus we attain a teleological standard of value, according to which things rank higher or lower as they attain to or recede from the final end of individuation.   This mixture of Hodgskin and Schelling (for so it may be regarded) furnishes the basis of Spencer's philosophy; and his later development consists in the progressive attempt to reconcile this basis with the data of natural science.

That natural science, however, was of the physical rather than the biological order. From early youth he had been interested in physics. He had loved air pumps and electrical machines ; he had even been a practising engineer for some years; and he had not loved or pursued the study of language or literature.   He was thus free from the " bias " towards custom and tradition; he was thus driven towards natural causation and natural law.   It was in this way that he came to give his book the title of *Social Statics*.   It is natural to suspect in this title the influence of Comte.   Comte had conceived sociology as the science of social physics, and had divided social physics into the two departments of statics and dynamics; and he had emphasised, like Spencer, the idea of social " laws."   But if it is natural, it is also erroneous.   Spencer knew nothing of Comte till after 1850.   The theological and metaphysical

assumptions of *Social Statics* are exactly what
Comte sought to eliminate from his positive
philosophy; and the scientific paternalism of
Comtist politics is the antipodes of Spencer.
Spencer is only indebted to Comte for a few
terms (such as *sociology*), and for the impulse to
define himself more clearly in opposition to
Positivism. At the same time, if his philosophy
did not become Comtian, it became more and
more a matter of physics. The development
is rapid till the beginning of 1858, when it
reaches its goal in the first draft of the *Synthetic
Philosophy*. A divine and transcendental idea
of life has now given place to force. There is
still the idea of universal evolution, but it is
now expressed in mechanical terms of force,
and not in organic terms of life. The first
principle is the Persistence of Force: issuing
from it are two main corollaries—the tendency
of all things to ultimate equilibrium, and the
consequent tendency of all things to transform
themselves by a process of evolution in order to
attain this equilibrium. All nature, including
human society as a part of nature, is bound together as one whole in a universal process of
transformation or evolution, which is the result
of a universal law of the equilibration of forces;
and both the transformation and the universal
law which is its source are corollaries from the
Persistence of Force. These views had already
been reached before Darwin enunciated his
doctrine; and thus Spencer came to " social
evolution " not from biology, and not from any
use of biological analogy, but from a sweeping
view of universal evolution expressed in terms
of physics: a view which included in its sweep

both sociology and biology, and indeed astro-
nomy and geology also, as all alike parallel
manifestations of the same law.

But biology had a peculiar influence on
Spencer's sociology. It is a mistake—for
which he chides Professor Giddings, who never
made the mistake—to suppose that Spencer
based sociology on biology; but it remains true
that the two are intimately and peculiarly connected in his theory. Spencer had been interested in biology ever since he bred insects as
a boy. As he advanced, he adopted, and
adapted to his system, the principles of biology
suggested by Lamarck as early as 1800. He
held, that is to say, that external environment
acts on living beings (a belief which Buckle's
History of Civilisation, published in 1856, may
have helped to fortify); that living beings
adapt their functions and structure to external
environment; and that such adaptation is inherited from generation to generation.

This marks a departure from the Coleridgean
view of the development of life *ab intra.* Such
development is now conceived, on the contrary,
to proceed *ab extra.* But the new view could
be and was subsumed under the old physical
law of universal evolution. Adaptation to
environment is simply a matter of equilibration
of forces or energies : it is an adjustment of
the energy of the living being to the energy of
the environment. Lamarck's biology, thus connected with universal physical evolution, leads
to Spencer's psychology and to his sociology.
Mind adjusts or equilibrates itself with external
environment by an adaptation of itself which
becomes its inherited tissue of tradition. The

individual, again, equilibrates himself with his
social environment by adaptation, and by inheritance of that adaptation, until he attains in
a perfect equilibrium the blessedness of final
anarchy. It is important to notice that Spencer
ended, as he began, in Lamarckianism of this
order. He never became a Darwinian. He
had finished his mental development, and had
sketched the plan of his *Synthetic Philosophy,*
some months before Darwin published his
theory. Darwin disbelieved in the doctrine of
purposive adaptation to environment : he believed in accidental variations, and held that
accidental variations which suited environment
were perpetuated by inheritance, ultimately because they were the fittest for that environment,
but immediately because they were inevitably
selected for survival in the course of the struggle
for life. Spencer was willing to admit natural
selection as a cause of " indirect equilibration,"
that is to say, as responsible for such cases of
equilibration of a living being with its environment as were not the effect of a direct reaction
by that being on its environment; he was even
willing to allow that in the earliest stages there
was more indirect than direct equilibration. In
other respects he was not a Darwinian; and
even in these respects he had already attained
his view independently of Darwin, and before
Darwin ever wrote. Already in *Social Statics,*
he recognises the " stern discipline of nature "
which eliminates the unfit and secures " the
maintenance of a constitution completely
adapted to surrounding conditions," and it is
in the name of such discipline that he attacks
the system of Poor Relief.

How did Spencer reconcile the idealist Idea
of Life from which he started with the material-
ist Persistence of Force in which he ended?
And how did he reconcile both with his early
radicalism, and its gospel of the natural rights
of the living individual? The first reconciliation was attained, or rather attempted, through
a vague use of the terms life and force, which
served to cover the change from a doctrine of
self-developing organisms to a doctrine of self-
equilibrating mechanisms. But this vagueness
only conceals a real irreconcilability; and the
real irreconcilability is shown in his political
theory by the perpetual variability of the conception of social organism. The social organism
will, as it were, constantly insist on coming to
life and on being a living substance; and Spencer
has to resort to far-fetched devices to kill it
again, in order to assert a mechanical conception of the state as a compound of physical
units. The chief device which he employs is a
distinction between two main stages of political
evolution, the military and industrial. To the
former and inferior stage he assigns the in-
tegrated organism; to the latter and superior the
differentiation of units—as if integration and
differentiation were not concomitant and correlative, and as if evolution could be chopped
with a hatchet into two dissimilar stages.
Another device, fundamentally the same, is to
distinguish between two kinds of integration,
that of status and that of contract (a distinction
borrowed from Maine), and then—relegating
status, which represents an organic condition,
to barbaric military days—to vindicate contract, which represents a mechanical connection,

for later industrial days—as if industrialism did
not necessarily involve the very highest degree
of organic interdependence.

The reconciliation of his Radical politics
with his general philosophy Spencer attained
by means of a cult of the Absolute, or of
Utopianism. His argument runs as follows.
Evolution, whether it be conceived as a tendency of life to individuation, or of forces to
equilibration, may be regarded as finally attaining a perfect equilibrium. This end,
which lies in the future, and may thus be regarded as a distant Utopia, constitutes an
absolute standard or norm. The perfect equilibrium (or if we translate this into Lamarckian
terms, the perfect adaptation), which evolution
will attain, represents the social ideal. Such
an ideal is necessarily static, because progress
stands still and movement ceases when such an
ideal is attained. Hence Spencer speaks of a
code of Social Statics, which he regards as the
standard of measurement, by which everything
must be judged and by the degree of its approximation to which everything must be valued.
But this is simply to repeat the old idea of
natural rights as a standard or norm of social
arrangement, with the one difference that the
code is translated into the future, and connected
with evolution. In the form which it takes in
Spencer, the doctrine of Natural Right is simply
a doctrine of the blessedness of final anarchy.
The perfect equilibrium or adaptation once
attained, man automatically does for himself
what he ought to do; and government will drop
away like a vesture. The ideal is thus anarchy;
and by the degree of its approximation to

anarchy we must value the worth of every
society. Such an idea is open to two criticisms.
In the first place, the evolution of human conduct never attains such a static repose. The
horizon always recedes : there is never a perfect and final adaptation ; each new adaptation
suggests a new set of problems, and leads to a
new adaptation. In the second place, Spencer
is apt to fall into confusions about the relation
between the final Utopian norm and the social
conditions of the present. Instead of holding
fast to the idea that the social conditions of a
given time are just, and perfectly good, so far
as they represent the best possible approximation to the ideal, he is apt to set such social conditions over against his ideal, and then to
criticise them by his ideal standard as imperfect
and unjust. However much he might urge
against critics of his " absolute ethics " that he
had recognised the value of existing social institutions, he really failed to do so—at any rate
in *Social Statics.* On the contrary, fixing his
eye on his final Utopia of Anarchy, he criticises
existing government as in its nature unjust;
and thus he falls into a curious mediævalism,
which sees in all government the product and
the author of evil and violence. Thus his conception of evolution, just because it postulates
a final end which is the standard of justice, is
reconciled with his Radical politics; but just
for that reason also his whole political theory
goes askew, because it tends to a view of government and social institutions as unjust and un-
justifiable. And thus again the living social
organism, his inheritance from early idealism,
is continually at war with the doctrine of in-

dividual natural rights, that inheritance from
a still earlier Radicalism which he afterwards
sought to justify by an eschatological conception of evolution.

We have spoken of Spencer's sources and his
debt to other thinkers. Spencer was himself
inclined to emphasise his own originality. In
a letter to Leslie Stephen in 1899 he asserts
that when he wrote *Social Statics* he had no
preparation : he looked at things through his
own eyes and not through the eyes of others :
he went straight to the facts, and drew his in-
ferences direct from life. The truth is, that he
read hastily and gained a number of rapid impressions, and that he often absorbed ideas
(notably from Hodgskin) in the course of con-
versation. Not having read systematically, he
thought that he was original, while all the time
he was at the mercy of hasty impressions
gathered in reading or in talk. With a positive
genius for generalisation (which led him at once
to brilliant discovery and astounding errors) he
attempted to synthesise this very imperfect
material. But he had not gone to the " facts "
in *Social Statics ;* and he did not go to the real
facts of the social structure of civilised life even
in his *Descriptive Sociology.* If he had worked
systematically at the thought of his predeces-
sors, and studied systematically the real facts,
he would have achieved less, and perhaps
helped the world more. As it is, we must consider him as a brilliant generaliser from imperfect data which he had never really thought
together into a unity. That is why the study of
his " sources " matters more for the under-
standing of Spencer than it does for the study
of most other thinkers.

We may now approach *Social Statics,* which Spencer published in 1850, remembering that it is a statement of the final static repose of society—of society as it should be in its absolute form, rather than as it actually is. Of actual government and its ways Spencer shows, here as elsewhere, a lively abhorrence. He brought this feeling from his " dissenting family, antagonistic," as he says, " to arbitrary control "; and living in an age which hoped for economic happiness from the repeal of governmental restrictions on trade, he was led to hope for universal happiness from the abolition of all government except the necessary policeman and the indispensable courts of law. The recurrent refrain of his writings, from first to last, is denunciation of the stupidity, the bungling, the red tape of government. Like Buckle, he delivers a perpetual commination service against the Sins of Legislators. And herein lies his bitter savour of truth. No one can read Spencer without learning a lesson which it is good to learn, that the State after all only acts through the finite intelligence of its officials. We must not expect more from it than we expect from our own equally finite intelligence. But Spencer is not content with this moral. He goes further. He urges that we may expect more from the intelligence of the individual than we can from the intelligence of the State and its officials. He opposes to the cult of the State the cult of the individual.

The obverse of his hostile attitude to the State is a belief in the natural rights of the individual. The fundamental thing in the world is the free exercise of individual capacity,

D

wherein alone lies the happiness ordained for
man by the Unknown Cause; and the fundamental first principle of *Social Statics,* from
which all else flows by deduction, is the law of
equal freedom, whereby, each individual attaining a freedom limited only by the necessity of
like freedom for others, the maximum of exercise of capacity, and thus of happiness, may be
attained. Spencer's individual is essentially
an unrelated and therefore unreal individual;
but it is on him that Spencer builds his whole
philosophy. He is quite clear in Social Statics
(and he repeats the dictum in the *Principles of
Sociology*) that if we would understand the
social aggregate, we have only to understand
the units of which it is an aggregate. The
characteristics of the associated State must be
the consequences of the " inherent properties "
of the associated individuals. The individual
may be regarded from two aspects, an outer
and an inner. In the former aspect he is a
being, with a faculty which demands freedom
as the condition of that adaptation to function
which constitutes perfection; in the latter he
is a consciousness, endowed with an inherent
sense of justice which makes him claim for
himself, and with a sympathetic affection
which makes him respect in others, the freedom
his faculty requires. In speaking of the outer
aspect of the individual Spencer expresses his
belief in that benevolence of nature and harmony of interests of which Adam Smith had
written. Nature has so wrought her plan, and
so adjusted every part to every other, that each
being can, by being itself and freely acting as
itself, best fit her plan and suit her adjustment.

His conception of the inner side of the individual is equally influenced by the teaching of the Scotch intuitional school, and especially of Adam Smith. He believes in an innate instinct of justice, and in that sympathetic affection of this instinct, termed beneficence, which makes every man spontaneously inclined to allow others to claim, and to support others in claiming, what he demands himself. Spencer indeed tells us that he learned this last doctrine of sympathy and beneficence from the study of phrenology, years before he knew of Adam Smith. Whatever its source, he definitely enounces in *Social Statics* those doctrines which Bentham had denounced. He opposes to the rational calculus of utility the doctrine of intuition. He holds that each consciousness is so constituted as spontaneously to adjust itself fully and adequately to all others.

Associate together these beings and their consciousnesses, and you get freedom—a freedom so far modified by the fact of association that it must be *equal* freedom for each member—as the one and only law of that association, from which all others flow, and to which all others must conform. Freedom is the antecedent of government : freedom is its standard. Thus we arrive at rights, which " are nothing but artificial divisions of the general claim to exercise the faculties." These rights, we perceive, are " natural," in the sense of pre-social right; they are " inherent properties " of the " human constitution as divinely ordained." We must not stay to slay the slain; we can only notice in passing that rights,

which cannot exist without social recognition,
are here divorced from that recognition, as
they must inevitably be by any thinker
who starts from unrelated individuals. We
must proceed to consider Spencer's notion
of the content of rights. Here we may distinguish the private rights of the citizen, which
are concerned more particularly with his property and his family; and his public rights,
which are concerned with his relations to the
State. Spencer's conception of private rights
has certain peculiarities, which are however
logically connected with his general attitude.
He disbelieves entirely in any right of private
property in land, because it contravenes the
law of equal freedom, which demands equal
access to the land. That law postulates public
and national ownership of the soil; but such
ownership once granted, there may and must
be private property in its products, not only
because the producer has mixed his labour with
the products, but because he has hired the soil
for a consideration from the community, and
has thus obtained a right which is valid "*because he obtained the consent of society* before
expending his labour." This last significant
phrase seems somewhat destructive of Spencer's
whole theory of natural rights. If a right so
elementary as that of property involves social
recognition, it is difficult to see how rights can
in their nature be independent of social recognition. The self-contradiction is the more
serious, as Spencer definitely speaks of the desire for property as " one of the elements of our
nature," and thus implicitly claims as natural a
right which he afterwards recognises as social.

But revolutionary as he is in his treatment of property (and indeed natural and non-social rights cannot but be subversive of society), he is still more revolutionary in his treatment of the family. Premising that all command or government is in its nature barbarous, and that the free individual is, as it were, the only civilised institution, he attacks the " subjection of women " nearly twenty years before Mill, and goes far beyond Mill in attacking the subjection of children. Not only should women receive the vote, but, in an ideal system of social statics, the family as an organisation of life and a discipline of character should disappear, and the law of equal freedom should be extended to children, whose rights are co-extensive with those of adults, and should not be nullified by parental coercion.

In discussing public rights Spencer starts from the assumption that government, a relic of the predatory state, is from an ideal point of view a vicious and immoral institution, which in all its actions must necessarily interfere with the free play of faculty. It is indeed necessary : if it is a relic of the predatory state, there are also other relics, and these need government for their cure. But it is a necessity which must be modest ; which must efface itself ; which must justify its existence by existing as little as possible. And this it can do in three ways. In the first place it can efface itself, for the sake of the law of freedom, by admitting the right of the citizen ' to ignore the State." It can, and it must, permit its citizens to abandon the benefits and throw off the burdens of citizenship. Dissent is already an ignoring of the State in

one matter, and that a vital matter : dissent
must be generalised. But the point of the
paradox somewhat disappears, when we remember that this is only an ideal principle, and
that it can only operate when society is ideal.
Spencer tantalises the individual with glimpses
of jewels of freedom, which he can only wear
in the days of perfection.   In the second place,
government can meet the demands of the law
of equal freedom, by admitting all its citizens
to an equal share in the imposition of all the restraints it imposes.   Unless all are thus admitted, there will be class-bias and class-
government : if all are thus admitted, that
danger does not disappear, but nevertheless we
may put our trust in the masses ; partly because
they are too disunited to combine in the pursuit
of class-interest ; partly, and still more, because
they have at least as much goodness and as
much good sense as the rest of the community.
In the third place the State must carefully de-
limit its function.   Nature tells us that one
organ can only have one function ; and the
verdict of this " first principle," the voice of
history, and the universal practice of men combine to prove that the one function of the State
is protection—administration of the law of
equal freedom—maintenance of natural rights.
The State is a " joint-stock protection-company for mutual assurance." Without and
apart from the State, I may have perfect freedom for nine years, and lose freedom and life
itself in the tenth ; within the State I am never
wholly free, and yet never wholly lose my freedom.   There is as much aggression on freedom
within the State as without the State ; for the

State is making its small aggressions daily. But the aggressions are better distributed and more tolerable; and I therefore insure myself with the State, though I know that I shall not gain, and that I shall suffer just the same amount of aggression, because I prefer the method of its distribution. In this somewhat negative sense I am protected; and for this protection, but for nothing else, I insure myself. If the State tries to give me more, which it can only do by taking more from me, in order to get the means for its gift, it breaks the " tacit agreement " we have made. And here we may already see, what in *The Man versus the State* becomes explicit, that Natural Rights necessarily involve Social Contract, whatever incidental and irrelevant mention of " social organism " may adorn the process of the argument.

Spencer's account of the function of the State is mainly an account of what the State ought not to do. It ought not to regulate industry; it ought not to establish a State-Church; it ought not to attempt colonisation. It ought not to give poor relief, or to undertake the care of public health; for in both ways it defeats the operation of the law of natural selection—a law which Spencer thus seems to have grasped already in 1850, some eight years before Darwin and Wallace communicated their papers to the Linnæan Society. Nor, again, must the State give education. The child has no right to it—for he can exercise his faculties without it; and the parent on the other hand *has* a right to buy all his commodities—his child's education as much as his

milk—by free purchase in an open market un-
controlled by any monopoly.   Moreover state-
education will be conservative in tendency
(though that is hardly our experience of its
working); and it will not diminish crime, or
help the State to discharge its true and proper
function of protecting its members from wrong,
since ignorance has no connection with crime
and wrong-doing.   Finally, the State must not
institute a public mint, or work a postal system,
or erect a lighthouse.   It has, in a word, no
business to interfere with the wise severity of
nature's discipline, which makes us better
when we do things for ourselves, and—what is
more—makes the things which we do for ourselves better done than those which the State
does for us.

Here we may end our account of the high *a
priori* element in Spencer.   It contains nothing
which is really new, but much that is as old as
the Middle Ages; and it combines, in a way
which would have appalled Bentham, the
Benthamite principle of happiness with those
doctrines of natural rights and of an intuitive
moral sense which Bentham denounced as
prime fallacies.   It seems difficult, after con-
sidering this mechanical logic of abstract deduction, to see where biology can enter; and
yet it already enters in *Social Statics* in very
interesting ways.   Early in the book Spencer
speaks not only of men, but of all organisms, as
tending, in virtue of an essential principle of
life, to find freedom for the exercises of their
faculties through adaptation to their environment; and later in the book he objects to poor
relief and to public sanitation because they

prevent such adaptation, interfering as they
do with that discipline which, in all animate
creation, tends by means of the struggle for life
to produce the survival of the fittest.   He does
not see in this struggle the cause of the perpetuation of favourable variations and of the
consequent origin of species.   But he has already borrowed from Coleridge, and ultimately
from Schelling, a theory of life which makes
the true "idea of life" consist in a tendency
to individuation, and degrees of value of life in
the progressive realisations of this tendency;
and this theory prepares the way for his subsequent conception of evolution as progress
from the undifferentiated and homogeneous to
the differentiated and heterogeneous.   It is his
belief in this principle of "individuation" which
inspires the warmth of his feeling for the individual.   It is from this point of view that he
can speak of morality as a species of transcendental physiology.   If a tendency to individuation is the law of all animate life, and if the
moral law is simply the rule for the individuation of human life through the free exercise
of individual capacity, it follows that the
moral law is a species of the universal law.   If
Spencer had stopped here he might have been
clear, if he was not correct.   We should have
had a theory of the world-process of individuation of organisms, in which the struggle for
life left as the survivors the most individuated
organism---the organism which showed the
most unique capacity working most freely in
virtue of the perfect harmony between itself
and its environment.

   But Spencer did not stop here.   He had

D 2

written of individuation, and had combined
a belief in individuation with a belief in the
individual and his rights. He had next to
think of society and its claims. He had to
think of the process of social individuation,
and of the relation of individual to social
individuation. He faced the problem, but
instead of solving it he hid his head in the
sands of metaphor. There is one individuation, he argued, of the individual; there is
also another individuation of society. The
result of the process, for both alike, is an
organism. There is an individual organism,
and there is a social organism; and the two
are parallel. Some obvious difficulties occur
to the mind. In the first place, to suggest
a parallel between two things is not to determine the relation between them. The more
you labour the parallel, the more you forget
to determine the relation. Spencer is the
classical instance of the labour and the forgetting. In the second place, if you seek to
establish a parallel, it is necessary to be clear
about the two terms of the parallel. If you
compare two organisms, you must be clear
about both. Spencer is clear about the individual organism, which is obviously physical;
he is by no means equally clear about the
social organism. To be intelligible, he must
mean by a social organism a mental system;
for a society is a union of minds to achieve a
common purpose. On the other hand, to be
consistent he must mean by a social organism
a physical system. What a physical social
organism may be it is very difficult to comprehend. And yet we shall find Spencer

THE SOCIAL ORGANISM   107

attempting to comprehend such a thing, and including in the social organism both railways and the telegraph wires which run by their side.

When we speak of an organism, we mean (1) a living structure composed of parts different in kind; (2) that those parts, by reason of their difference, are complementary to one another and mutually dependent; (3) that the health of the whole consequently depends on the healthy discharge by each part of its own proper function. An organism thus possesses the correlative attributes of a high degree of differentiation and a high degree of integration; and " organic unity " means unity in and through difference. Again, an organism, just because it is a living structure, and just because it works so subtly through the reciprocal functions of its parts, cannot be changed from without by any mechanical act. It grows; it grows from within by a development which affects all its parts simultaneously; and such growth is what is called " organic growth." Now all these terms—organism, organic unity, organic growth—may be, *by a metaphor*, applied to the State. The State is not an organism; but it is like an organism. It is not an organism, because it is not a physical structure. It is a mental structure—a union of different minds in a common purpose. But this mental structure is like an organism, because (1) the attainment of the common purpose depends on the discharge of reciprocal functions by the different parts, and the unity of the structure is thus " organic "; and

(2) any change of the structure can only come
from within, and by way of a development
affecting all the parts together, and the
growth of the structure is thus " organic."
The fact, however, remains, that the State is
not an organism, because it is a self-determining system of minds which are themselves
self-determining; and the whole analogy
leads to confusion instead of clearness, unless
we are clear about the terms of the comparison, and unless we are also clear that
metaphor is not argument, and that a parallel
between the State and the individual is not an
explanation of their relation.

In *Social Statics* Spencer has already begun
to speak of a " social organism." The development of society, he says, may be conceived as
the result of a tendency to individuate and
become a thing. What he never explains is
how the State can tend to become a thing, and
how an individual supposed to be utterly and
entirely opposed to it can tend to become a
thing within it, at one and the same time.
That problem—and after all it is the fundamental problem of political theory—demands
for its solution a full and just conception of
the individual, which abolishes the supposed
opposition between the man and the State,
and recognises that the individual has for the
highest element of his individuality an element
of reason and rational purpose which is common to him with others and the bond of his
communion with others   For want of such a
conception, and lacking as he does any real
theory of the relation of the individual
mind to the social system of minds, Spencer

can in the same treatise, and within a few
pages, speak of the State first as a joint-stock
protection-company, and then as a social
organism. " An uncriticised individualism,"
as Prof. Bosanquet says, " is always in
danger of transformation into an uncritical
collectivism." If you do not grasp your
" individual " firmly, he slips round in your
hands, and you find you have hold of him
as it were at the other end. He will insist,
that is to say, on showing his social aspect, and
on becoming " common." You find, as Spencer
finds and urges at the end of *Social Statics*, that
" human progress is· towards greater mutual
dependence, as well as towards greater individuation "; " the welfare of each is involved in the welfare of all "; " all men's
business in the business of each." And so the
book which tells us to start from the unit, and
to see in the whole the mere result of its inherent properties, ends by telling us that the
health of the social organism " in a measure "
depends on the fulfilment of some function in
which the unit takes part, and that the happiness of each unit depends on the normal action
of every organ in the social body. Surely
there is some inconsistency here. And if we
try to answer that charge by pleading that
it is *government*, to which the individual is
opposed, and *society* in which he has a function,
we shall hardly succeed by that answer.
Government is part of society and one of its
organs : how can it be in its nature opposed
to the rest? If, again, we plead that government is a " deciduous organ," a relic of the
predatory state, which is a nuisance and an

anachronism in the industrial State, we shall hardly succeed any more. The industrial State does require government—government more multifarious and pervasive than any before. The " deciduous organ," as a matter of fact, has never been more vigorous than it is to-day.

A quarter of a century passed before Spencer published his next consecutive treatise on politics—the *Principles of Sociology,* of which the first volume appeared in 1876. This period was largely occupied by the development of his general philosophy, but it is also marked by a number of articles on political subjects, mostly in the *Westminster Review,* of which the most important are reprinted in the three volumes of his *Essays.* In some matters Spencer changes, in others he continues, the lines of *Social Statics.*

The change is partly one of general attitude, partly one of particular tenets. An increasingly mechanical conception of the world displaces the old conceptions of divine guidance and intuitive moral ideas. The *Principles of Psychology* of 1855 show Spencer admitting the outer world of environment into the mind, and regarding human faculties as " organised results of the intercourse between the organism and the environment," which are transmitted from generation to generation by inheritance. More striking is the change in Spencer's attitude to the particular problems of land and the position of women. This change presents some difficulties and some amusement. Spencer had a vanity which, as it made him concerned about his originality, made him also concerned about his consistency. He was not sufficiently frank; when he shifted his ground, he was apt to cover up his tracks to conceal the change; and a habit of taking refuge from the stress of controversy in a sort of sulky silence did not conduce to light. He was thus involved in difficulties with Mill and Helen Taylor about Woman's Suffrage (1867), and with Henry George about Land Nationalisation (1882); and the difficulties on the latter question afterwards led to strained relations with Huxley (1889–1893) and to a quarrel with Henry George (1893–1896). The fact was that Spencer modified, and did not frankly admit that he had modified, his old views on these subjects; and this is amusingly illustrated in the edition of *Social Statics* of 1892, which omits the relevant passages of the first edition without any explanation. No wonder Mill and Henry George claimed his alliance, and were surprised to find it was not theirs; no wonder the keen controversialist Huxley rallied Spencer on his tergiversation, and was surprised to find that he retired into silent pique. The difficulty sprang from the fact that there was from the first a confusion in *Social Statics* between the absolute or Utopian ideal and actual social institutions. It was not clear to which department woman's suffrage and land nationalisation belonged. Mill and Henry George claimed them for actual social institutions; Spencer, alarmed to find his Utopia coming so close ("I had no conception that the question would be raised in our time, but had in thought a distant future"), sought to banish it into the far future. And he did this the more anxiously because, as we shall see, he had come to recognise that social institutions, as they stand, have a relative justification, as the proper forms of equilibration for their own age and stage of growth, and that they must not be, as in *Social Statics* they tend to be, rejected or even despised in comparison with the absolute ideal.

If in these respects the lines of *Social Statics* are abandoned between 1850 and 1875, in many respects they are continued, and even enriched and developed. The essay on *The Theory of Population* (1852) urges that decrease of fertility accompanies higher development, because the individuation which this brings is antagonistic to reproduction. The article on the *Art of Education* (1854), afterwards embodied in the short treatise on *Education* (1861), regards education in something of the old way, as essentially a process of self-development, on the ground that "humanity has progressed solely by *self*-instruction." Above all, the notion of the social organism was developed, partly in the Essay on *The Social Organism* (1860), and partly in that on *Specialised Administration* (an answer to Huxley's Essay on *Administrative Nihilism*) in 1871. In *Social Statics* the analogy (" we may almost say there is more than analogy ") between the State and the living organism had been mainly urged on the ground that both were commonwealths of parts with reciprocally subservient functions, parts so closely united that none of them could ever be injured without detriment to all the rest. Again, assuming that the

degree of differentiation represented the scale
of value, Spencer had also urged that the
analogy could be applied historically and
qualitatively; that the low form of State
with little differentiation of function could be
assimilated to the low form of organism with
its low degree of differentiation, and the high
form of State with the greatest articulation
of parts to the high form of organism with the
maximum of differentiation. The Essay on
The Social Organism is meant to emphasise a
different point. Here Spencer insists that
society is like an organism because it " grows
and is not made "; and he points the moral
that it should be left " to grow " under the
free play of social influence, and not " made,"
or rather checked and hindered, by governmental regulation. This was the point intended, and this is the strain on which the
essay begins; but the conception of social
organism is two-edged, and it tends to cut the
opposite way when the end of the essay is
reached. An organism is a unity with a
nerve-centre; that nerve-centre regulates the
whole body; and thus of a sudden the " growing " organism which should not be regulated
becomes a bureaucratic or socialistic state under
the control of the central brain. Starting
with a conception of organic growth intended
to justify individualism, Spencer ends with
a conception of organic unity which tends
to justify socialism. Huxley, with his keen
eye, fixed on this inward contradiction in his
essay on *Administrative Nihilism* (1870);
and Spencer, both in his reply in *Specialised
Administration* in 1871, and in all his later

political writings, is occupied in reconciling the contradiction.

In 1876 Spencer published the first volume of *The Principles of Sociology*, the next great landmark after *Social Statics* in the development of his political theory. The way had been prepared by a large collection of data, the *Descriptive Sociology*, begun in 1867 (and not yet completed), which reminds us of the descriptions of 158 constitutions which Aristotle collected to form the basis of his *Politics*. The *Principles of Sociology* emphasise the doctrine of the social organism, though with sufficient reservations to safeguard very amply natural rights, just as *The Man Versus the State*, some ten years later, emphasises natural rights, though with sufficient references to biology to safeguard, if less amply, the doctrine of the social organism. The purpose, therefore, of the *Principles* is to adopt where it is useful, and to reject where it is not, the organic conception of the State. The adoption seems whole-hearted : it is illustrated by a wealth of analogy, whether between Protozoa and Bushmen, or between the nerve-trunks running by the side of the arteries and the telegraph-wires which run by the side of railways. But the adoption is only secured at the cost of a sacrifice of the unity of the organism. The natural organism, we are told, contains two organisations. There are the organs of the nervous system, which form the apparatus of external action; there are the organs of the alimentary or sustaining system, concerned with the assimilation of food. The first set of organs is under the strict and despotic control of the regulating

brain, as it must necessarily be in order to
meet external needs with efficiency : the
second set of organs has a regulating system
of its own, which is no way despotic, but is
based on the sympathetic affection and the
mutual influence of the co-operating parts.
Not only are the alimentary organs independent
inter se ; they are practically independent of
the first set of organs and its regulating brain.
At the very most the " higher " or nervous
system only " restrains " the " lower " or
alimentary system; it sees that the organs
of alimentation are paid in exact proportion
to the work which they do. Now all this is
true, *mutatis mutandis*, of the social organism.
It has two organisations. There are the
organs of the governmental system, which
serve for external action ; there are the organs
of the industrial system, which serve for
internal life. The former involve despotic control to meet the needs of war from which they
spring : the latter constitute a self-controlling
co-operative system. The industrial system
(which Spencer makes the " higher," at the
cost of falsification of his analogy) is practically independent of the governmental system ;
at most it needs a " negative regulation " by
that system. It only needs such restraint as
will secure that none of its parts shall get
alimentation without doing work; it needs, in
a word, the enforcement of contracts which
determine the proportion between work and
alimentation. Thus government exists externally for war, and internally for the enforcement of contracts. It has no further *raison
d'être* or function. It must leave aside posi-

tive regulation; it must specialise exclusively
on negative regulation in order to discharge
efficiently its one and only function. This is
what Spencer means by " specialised administration."

The argument seems neat, and the analogy
close. But it contains difficulties, and Spencer
was not unaware of those difficulties. Even
if the stomach pursues a sort of independent
existence in the body, it is not the end of the
body, or even the higher part of the body.
But industrial society, which corresponds to
the stomach, *is* the end of the body politic,
or at any rate its higher part. To solve the
difficulty Spencer has recourse to a fundamental distinction between the social and the
natural organism. The one is discrete; the
other is concrete. There is no social sensorium,
or single centre of consciousness; each member
of society is, what each part of a natural
organism is not, an organ of feeling and
thought. Since there is no social sensorium,
it follows that the happiness of the aggregate
is not the end; since the centres of consciousness are local and individual, it follows that
their local and individual happiness is the end.
Thus a society which acts on the theory that
the individual is a means to the happiness of
the aggregate, as every military society does,
is a wrong and " low " society; a society which
acts on the theory that the happiness of the
individual is an end to which government is
a means, as the later industrial society does,
is a right and " high " society. Or, putting it
in another way, we may say that the regulating
governmental system of organs, which origin-

ated in war, is necessarily based on the assumption of despotic control of each individual for the sake of success in war, and thus sacrifices the individual, and thus again falls low in the scale of value, since individual happiness is the end and therefore the standard of value; while the sustaining industrial system of organs, which originates in the peaceful pursuit of individual wealth, is based on the opposite assumption, and thus realises the individual, and thus again stands high in the scale of value. On all this it follows that while the evolution of the animal organism is towards the triumph of the nervous system, the evolution of the social organism is towards the triumph of the alimentary system. But if this is so, the stomach is, after all, the end of the social organism.

Having thus inverted the order of value—having made the industrial system the "higher" system in the social organism—Spencer proceeds to show a historical process making for the triumph of industrial society. That process starts from a *Kriegstaat*, where all is war, and there is no industry; where all men are strictly regulated by government as means to its end; where, all men being thus held to their places, status is the consequent rule. The process ends in a *Handelstaat*, where all is industry and there is no war; where all men, as ends in themselves, are knit by voluntary association; where contract is the rule of industry, and colours by sympathetic affection the rest of life. It inspires politics, and creates democracy; it inspires religion, and creates a system of free churches; it inspires social life, and produces voluntary education and voluntary charity. The Utopian ideal of *Social Statics* has returned again, but in the somewhat lower and commercialised form of an industrial society. The old contrast between ideal anarchy and actual social institutions is now a contrast between the military State and industrial society; and sometimes it even appears as a contrast between the Tory party, with its cult of militarism and status, and the Liberal party—the old and true Liberal party, and not the new Radical perversion—with its cult of industrialism and contract.

The whole argument suggests several reflections. In the first place the social organism is only saved by being cut in pieces. It is only reconciled with the individualism of industrial society by a distinction between the discreteness of the social organism and the concreteness of the natural organism which destroys the whole notion of a social organism. And so it is no wonder to find that, in spite of a hundred pages of analogy, Spencer ultimately bows the social organism out of doors. He is not content with cutting it in pieces; he sends it into exile. It has served as a " framework " for building a true structure; but the structure is " independent " of it. In the second place Spencer's bifurcation of State and society cannot stand. We may distinguish State and society, as Hegel and Bosanquet, in different ways, seek to do; what we cannot do, and what neither Hegel nor Bosanquet attempts to do, is to bifurcate the two. Society is held together by the State; and if it were not thus held together, it could not exist.   It is easy to say, with Spencer, that voluntary co-operation achieves the vast mass of the world's work, and that the State (in the sense of the government) achieves but little, and that little ill.   It is harder, but it is very necessary, to see that voluntary co-operation is only made possible by the State, and, what is more, that the more there is of voluntary co-operation, the more need there is of the State.   But that is the simple fact.   The State, as the great source of adjustment, is all the more needed the more there is to adjust.   One has only to look the facts in the face to see that the great extension in modern times of voluntary co-operation, both between master and man, and between master and master, also meant a great extension of government.   Government has had to keep pace with industry : government has had to solve its problems by Factory Acts, Company Acts, and Acts innumerable.   In the third place one must admit that the Spencer of the *Principles of Sociology* has made some progress since he wrote *Social Statics*.   There he was prone to reject, or at any rate to despise, social institutions :   in the *Principles* he acknowledges that institutions have a relative justification.   His semi-historical idea of the nature of primitive predatory society helped Spencer to make this advance.   Many things may be admissible, he came to believe, *so long as militancy is great*.   Moreover, the material accumulated in the pages of *Descriptive Sociology* modified to some extent his old " repugnance to coercion," his old " abhorrence of

slavery," his old " aversion to ecclesiasticism."
It showed the need, for their own day and in
their own time, of strong kingship; of slavery
as a method of cultivation and a means of
leisure; and even of supernatural control.
Perhaps " relative justification of social institutions " is only a long name for the simple
fact of a growing Conservatism, already evident
in the attitude of his later days to questions
like land nationalisation and woman's suffrage;
and many will prefer the impossible Radicalism
of Spencer at the age of thirty to the doctrine
of relative justification which he attained as
he neared the age of sixty.

The *Principles of Sociology* starts from
the social organism, but ends in Natural
Rights : *The Man versus the State* (1884)
starts from and ends in Natural Rights.
Natural rights, after all, are the solid core of
Spencer's thought. The reasons lie deep.
They are to be found not only in those particular
influences of his early life, of which we have
already spoken, but also in the elementary
fact that Spencer was an Englishman, and
that Englishmen cannot easily get away from
a belief in natural rights. Two causes have
contributed to this national characteristic, the
one religious, the other economic. The one is
Dissent : the other is the doctrine of laissez-
faire. Dissent, on the whole a peculiarly
English phenomenon, is the primary source.
Spencer was himself sprung from the ranks of
Dissent, and in *Social Statics* he couples with a
reference to the history of Dissent his advocacy
of the " right to ignore the State." In the
history of Dissent the Independents are of

particular importance. They asserted not only
the independence of the religious conscience
from the control of the State, but also the
independence of the individual congregation
from any ecclesiastical organisation; and
Green has remarked how in the younger Vane,
the recognised representative of Independency,
there first appears in England the doctrine
of natural rights. A little later, and we have
in Locke a philosophy which we may almost
say that Independency has made possible—a
philosophy of the limited function of the
State, based on the assumption of the natural
rights of independent man. Another and later
development reinforced the idea which had
thus found its origin in religion. This development is the political economy of Adam Smith
and his successors. Of this development we
shall have to speak later in its proper connection; it is sufficient here to notice that the
economic right of the individual was now
added to his religious right, so that Spencer
can constantly couple the idea of natural
rights with the idea of industrial society. It
is little wonder, in the light of these facts, that
the idea of natural rights should have been
continuously, if often unconsciously, cherished
by generations of Englishmen. Englishmen,
it is often said, have always appealed not to
the general natural rights of all men, but to
the peculiar legal rights of Englishmen. As a
matter of fact the Englishmen of the seven-
teenth century could openly appeal to natural
rights; and whether the appeal has been
openly made or no, the idea has served as a
motive force, and it is still a motive force—

nowhere more striking than in some of the
agitations of recent years—in modern England.
It is the merit of Spencer's severe logic that he
brings into the open daylight what is lurking
at the back of most men's minds.

In laying down the doctrine of Natural Rights
in *The Man versus the State* Spencer alleges
as its source and its support the science of life.
The " science of life " has a biological sound;
but all that Spencer means is an *a priori* view
of human nature. If we look at the life of
the individual on the assumption that it is
worth living, he argues, we must conclude
that the acts necessary for its maintenance
are right, and the claims and liberties necessary
to those acts are rights. It may be urged in
reply, as it is by Huxley, that on this argument
tigers have their rights. No, rejoins Spencer; there is a difference between the rights
of man and the rights of the tiger. The
presence and society of other men constitute
this difference. Man must not claim (but
Spencer gives no explanation *why* he must
not claim) any rights of action which interfere
with his fellows' rights of action. And if man
thus abandons some of his claims and liberties,
the rest of his claims and liberties may be
regarded as *ethical* rights. One can only reply
that if they are regarded as ethical rights,
there are no more natural rights, and there
is a great confusion of thought. But Spencer
now turns, leaving confusion as it stands, to
the science of the life of the society, as if it
were something different from the theory of
rights. He discovers that the conditions of
such life, based as it is on division of labour,

are freedom to make contracts of exchange and the enforcement of such contracts. And thus, he says, " it results that to recognise and enforce the rights of individuals is at the same time to recognise and enforce the conditions to a normal social life : there is one vital requirement for both." The State must confine itself to enforcement of contracts, otherwise it violates liberty, which " consists in the relative paucity of the restraints " which the State imposes on the rights of the individual. If the State attempts paternal government, it is introducing family-ethics into a domain to which they do not belong, and in which they will do untold harm. Family-ethics are based on the principle that benefits shall be given out of all proportion to desert; State-ethics are based on a rigorous justice, which, by enforcing contracts of exchange, ensures that each gets benefits exactly proportioned to his deserts, receiving in proportion as he gives, and giving in proportion as he receives. Family-ethics applied to the State would stop the beneficent struggle for existence, into which the citizen entered when he put away childish things; it would give the weakling more than he deserved and perpetuate an undeserving life. The phrase, and indeed the whole argument, raises difficulties. How can the State tell, and what criterion can it use to discover, what life is undeserving? The search for such a criterion is the difficulty that confronts those Eugenists who advocate artificial selection. But it is also a difficulty which the believer in unchecked natural selection has to face. If he assumes that the life which

cannot find means of subsistence is undeserving,
he has indeed something of a criterion; but
that criterion belongs to the sphere of " tiger-
rights," and not to the sphere of " ethical "
rights. A tiger has a right to do anything
in order to live; but man's rights, we have
just been told, are restricted by the presence
of his fellows, and are only " ethical." A tiger
has a " duty " to die when he cannot find food,
because he has the right to do anything in
order to find it; but has a man, with a restricted and " ethical " right, the like duty to
die? *Vix sequitur*. Has the State, then, any
duty to keep him alive, or to help him to
better conditions of living? At any rate, if
its existence restricts his " rights," there seem
to be the elements of such an obligation.

Spencer's supposed natural rights (it is difficult to see how on his own showing they are
really natural) carry him logically into the
doctrine of a social contract. It is true that
he attacks that doctrine in *Social Statics :*
it is true that even in *The Man versus the State*
he castigates " the error that society is a
manufacture; whereas it is a growth." He
can see that the conception of society as a
manufacture is responsible for the sins of
legislators; for it sets them manufacturing,
and manufacturing, in the nature of the case,
very badly. He even urges strongly the vital
connection between institutions and national
character, because he wishes to drive home
strongly the lesson that you can do no more
with institutions than national character allows
you, and that if it does not support and indeed
create an institution, the institution cannot work.

Nevertheless, natural rights *will* have their way. There must needs be some compact of the individual possessors of such natural rights before we can have a society : there must needs be some act of agreement to the restriction of natural rights before we can attain the ethical law of *equal* freedom. Already in *Social Statics* Spencer argues that, citizenship being willingly assumed (for the citizen has the right to ignore the State if he will), " there is an agreement tacitly entered into between the State and its members." Similarly, in *The Man versus the State*, after dismissing the baseless hypothesis of an actual contract, an hypothesis which, as a matter of fact, few thinkers have ever made, he finds a hypothetical contract nevertheless necessary. To find a moral origin alike for the institution of sovereignty and its limitation, " we ask what would be the agreement into which citizens would now enter with practical unanimity." In reality it is with the limitation of sovereignty rather than with its institution that Spencer, like Locke, is concerned. And therefore, after dismissing Quakers, who will hardly consent to war, and criminals, who will hardly consent to police, he defines the functions of the State as defensive war and defence against internal enemies. To these he adds, remembering his former advocacy of the national ownership of land, the use and control of the national territory—a vague phrase that only serves to cover the nakedness of his change of mind.

The hypothetical citizen who makes the hypothetical contract is really a prosperous business man, concerned for the protection

of his property and the free acquisition of land
for new premises and for the better transit
of his goods. He is the abstraction of the
economists; and whatever the value of economic
man for the economist, who has isolated for
inquiry the study of economic phenomena,
" economic man " will hardly serve as a
postulate for the political theorist, who has to
study the *citizen*, and to study him as a whole
in all his relations. We may assume the
" economic man " to have perfect insight into
his economic interest; but we cannot assume
the citizen to have anything like the same
quality of perfection. The perfect insight of
the economic man is of course an abstraction,
like the straight line of Euclid, but it is near
enough to serve its purpose; the perfect citizen
—too perfect to need more than a minimum
of State-action—is a flat contradiction of life.
Experience shows to us all, as we have seen
that it showed to Green, fellow-citizens of very
various degrees; and it shows us no small
number—labourers on the verge of subsistence, overworked women, denizens of London
yards—who can only enjoy Spencer's law of
equal freedom when the State by every manner
of " interference " has removed the obstacles
from their path. Here we may see the error
into which we are betrayed if, like Spencer,
we urge that " Social Science," like mechanical
and geometrical science, must work with perfect data—straight lines, " straight men." It
may logically do so, if it recognises that the
resultant structure will be a " straight " polity,
an ideal State; but it will be illogical, if it
seeks to apply to the crooked man, who after

all is what we have with us, the rules of the
" straight " State. The result is simply to
strengthen the hands of Conservatism or even
reaction. When the strict theorist urges that
" the State " (under which unqualified term
he confuses together the State of straight men
and the State of crooked men) ought not to do
so-and-so, or ought even to stop doing so-and-
so, he is doing exactly what the Conservative
and the reactionary desire.

Thus Spencer, just because he was too Radical, and too much a man of " first principles "
and " straight lines," ended in the Conservative
camp. The passage to the Conservative camp
was becoming general at the time when *The
Man versus the State* was published (1884).
Maine's *Popular Government*, which appeared
in 1885, is significant of the trend of thought.
Many were alarmed by the rapid progress
of Gladstonian Liberalism; and not a few
were so much alarmed by the progress of the
cause that they threw the cause overboard.
Nevertheless, it seems curious, at any rate
prima facie, to see the doctrine of natural
rights, so long connected with the Radicalism
of Tom Paine, becoming the corner-stone of
alarmed Conservatism. In reality the doctrine
may be used to support either cause indiffer-
ently. Natural Rights are the sand of refuge
in which the individual buries his head to
escape a pursuing State. They may serve
Conservatism for a refuge against a democratic and progressive State, no less than they
served the Whigs of 1688 for a defence against
the despotism of James II, or the Radicals of
1789 for a bulwark against a Whig oligarchy.

None the less, as Ritchie says, the ghost of Tom Paine must have chuckled when Lord Halsbury could tell a Conservative audience that "one of the things which the British people most cherished was their own freedom of action, the right to do as they willed with their own, whether it was their labour, their property, or their skill."

But we do Spencer an injustice. *He* had not changed in 1884. He had preached natural rights from the beginning; and it was the change of political conditions which made him the prophet of a different cause. It was the Tory party that had changed, or at any rate seemed to change, from the champion of paternalism against all manner of dissenters to the champion of individualism against all manner of socialists. Spencer was always the consistent advocate of an *a priori* individualism; and the inconsistency which he betrayed was not an inconsistency between what he held at one time and what he held at another, but an inconsistency between the two discrepant elements in his permanent theory, which he held together all along in an unreconciled antinomy—the element of individual rights and the element of social organism. He learned something in after life from natural science, but he never learned enough to conquer the unscientific principles from which he started. If natural selection suited his book, the social organism was not so complaisant. It wages a truceless war in the multitudinous pages of his writings with the idea of natural rights. That idea was already confused in itself, apart from the idea of the social organism. Spencer now urges that natural rights inhere in the individual, and now allows that they need the consent of society; at one time he holds that the rights of man belong to the law of all life as such, and at another he confesses that they differ from other rights in being ethical. The entry of the social organism makes confusion worse confounded; for natural rights in a social organism are as much in place as a vacuum in a solid. The tragedy is that if Spencer could only have been clear about rights, he would have made himself still clearer by his analogy of the social organism. As it stands, his philosophy of rights may be summarised in two contradictory propositions. (1) My rights, and all my morality, are positive and natural forces, springing from the *aviditas vitæ* and the love of self-assertion which I possess in common with all animate existence. (2) Since I am a man, living in the presence of my fellows, my rights are negative and ethical ideas, in the sense that they are not the fruit of self-assertion, but demand at any rate so much self-renunciation as will lead me to respect the rights of my fellows. If we abandon this self-contradictory hypothesis, and start from a will towards the good which I have in common with all other men, and in virtue not of my animality, but of my humanity—if we hold that rights spring from this moral good, peculiar to humanity, but common to humanity—then we see that rights are always positive in the sense that they rest on our nature as moral beings and on its impulse to assert itself as such, and that they are always just for that reason ethical; and we can also

E

see that they involve a social organism, because the good which is their source is common, and can best be attained in common.

Here we must leave the political philosophy of a thinker, who has probably had a greater vogue than any other in the last sixty years. No doubt that vogue has been due to the appearance of logic and synthetic system which pervades his writings; but it has been helped as much, or more, by the fact that his philosophy accords with an instinct for individual rights which the course of English history has made almost universal in England. Spencer's philosophy seems to set the stamp of authority on the *prima facie* philosophy of the ordinary man; and the ordinary man would not be ordinary if he did not like to see his views signed, sealed and delivered by a philosopher. Nor is Spencer's vogue altogether unconnected with his vocabulary. His writings abound in a facile terminology which, while only naming the problems to be solved, seems in itself to afford a solution; and the would-be learner always receives such a terminology with gladness, particularly when the terms are long. Moreover, there is a certain Puritanism in Spencer which was bound to attract attention and admiration in England. There is a fine air in *Social Statics* of *fiat justitia, ruat cœlum*. There is an atmosphere of stern, unbending rectitude. " This is the right thing on first principles, the only ultimate right, and the only real right. Imperfect man may not attain unto it; but it is the right." We are somewhat prone as a nation to a certain disjunction between a lofty moral theory and a somewhat more lowly practice. This is why we are sometimes called hypocrites abroad, and why our own literature, as it holds the mirror up to nature, presents with figures of hypocrites from Dickens to Meredith. Perhaps this national tendency to disjunction helped to give some of his vogue to Spencer, who was equally disjointed, and fell into some disingenuousness when he had to descend from the mountain heights of absolute right to practical questions like land-nationalisation and woman's suffrage. On the whole Spencer suited England; and on the assumption that a nation deserve the political theory which it gets, we may say that England deserved Spencer.

CHAPTER V

THE SCIENTIFIC SCHOOL—AFTER SPENCER

FROM first to last Spencer sought, however unsuccessfully, to bring politics into connection with biology. The two proved unwilling yoke-fellows; and Spencer is sometimes driven to take them out of double harness, and to make them run separately. Biology, he confesses, deals with organic evolution, while sociology deals with " super-organic " ; biology treats of the simple action of individual organisms, but sociology has to face the super-added factor of " co-ordinated action of many individuals." The cleavage between sociology and biology leads Spencer, at the end of the first volume of the *Principles of Sociology*, to draw a distinction between the social organism and the living organism, and to find in the discreteness of the one, and the concreteness of the other, the reason for a fundamental distinction between the two. The cleavage widens further in *The Man versus the State*. The little word " super " begins to involve large consequences. The additional factor of co-ordination, we now discover, makes man and his rights something different from animals and their rights. Man's rights, to be " ethical," have to be adjusted to suit the fact of co-ordination; " the presence of our fellows " constitutes a limit, and our rights only become just rights when they have been adjusted to that limit. And thus Spencer ends in an antithesis between the life-process of the natural world, in which each unit pushes as far as it can its right of individual self-assertion, and the ethical process of human society, in which each unit co-ordinates itself with others by renouncing self-assertion. Yet at the same time, however inconsistently, he still speaks of struggle, selection, and survival of the fittest as the laws of society.

The antithesis between natural and social right which is present even in Spencer is the dominant element in Darwin, in Huxley and in Russel Wallace. The life-process of cosmic nature, they all feel, is *not* like the ethical process of human society. By Darwin himself his great discovery of natural selection, though suggested to his mind by Malthus, a writer on social phenomena, was scarcely applied to society, or used to sanction any dogma of the natural right of man to struggle or of the natural duty of the State to confine itself to holding the ring. He felt indeed that natural selection had been an important in-

fluence in human history, because it had produced those social instincts, necessary to the
cohesion and therefore to the survival of each
tribe, which were the basis for the development
of the moral sense; and he felt that it was still
an important influence in modern societies, because the struggle for existence (or, as Huxley
would say, for the *means* of existence) was a
check on indolence and a guarantee of the success of the most gifted in the unending battle
of life.   But he thought that for man's highest
nature other agencies were more important,
and that moral qualities were much more
advanced by habit, reason, instruction and
religion than by natural selection.   On the
whole, Darwin devoted his thought to natural
science, and never set himself up to provide a
social philosophy.   What has happened to his
doctrine is that would-be social philosophers
have pressed it willy-nilly into their service;
and in this way it has been enlisted under
the different banners of anti-clericalism and
imperialism, socialism and militarism.

By Huxley social philosophy is explicitly
made something distinct from and indeed
opposite to natural science.   He starts, somewhat like Hobbes, from a contrast between
cosmic nature, with its " natural rights " of
self-assertion and self-satisfaction pursued
through cruel and unending struggle, and the
ethical nature of social men, aggregated in
societies whose end is the good of mankind,
and possessing social rights which are relative
to and controlled by this good.   The natural
order of things does not tend to bring about
the good of mankind; " cosmic nature," he

writes in *Evolution and Ethics*, " is no school of
virtue, but the headquarters of the enemy of
ethical nature."   Nature, red in tooth and claw
with ravin, is the realm of " tiger-rights " : she
plunges her creatures in a struggle for life, in
which natural selection secures survival not for
the morally best, or even for those who are absolutely the physically fittest, but simply and solely
for those who are the best adapted to the conditions which hold good in a given period—in
other words, for those who in some one respect,
and in that respect alone, are relatively fittest.
Nature knows no morals and no moral standard ;
her " fittest " are measured by no canon of
absolute worth, but by the relative canon of
adaptation to conditions; and nature's fittest
will be low in any human scale of values if
the conditions prevalent are low conditions.
Nature, again, knows no rights that *ought* to
be : her " rights " are simply the powers which
each of her creatures actually uses for its assertion of itself in struggle; and Nature simply
recognises by the grant of survival the power
which is most powerful under her given conditions.   Her " laws " are simply statements of
cruel facts : her rights are simply brutal
powers.   To import moral rights of freedom or
equality into this sphere is meaningless.   No
such rights exist in such a sphere; and any
notion of moral right must be set aside as irrelevant.   There is no freedom in a sphere where
you must adapt yourself or die; there is no
equality in a realm where the whole hypothesis
of survival of the fittest implies inequality.
  It is man who measures things as high or low
by a moral scale : it is man who says that the

higher ought to be : it is in the " artificial "
moral world created by man that morality
exists, and rights, in any other sense than
powers of ravin, have their being. Man is an
animal under the sway of Nature; but it is
his glorious and miserable destiny to be an
eternal rebel. He is Nature's slave and
Nature's master, and this is his unending
tragedy. He sees a world in which the action
of each individual is directed to the benefit of
that individual at the expense of all others :
he constructs a world whose end is the good
of mankind. For self-assertion he substitutes
self-restraint; in place of competition, he
requires that each shall " not merely respect,
but shall also help his fellows "; he sets his
face " not so much to the survival of the
fittest, as to the fitting of as many as possible
to survive." He arrests the cosmic process of
struggle in the interests of an ethical process
directed to the survival of those who are
ethically the best. He does not indeed go as
far as the horticulturalist with his plants, or
seek positively to breed the best; he has not
the necessary wisdom to select the best stock,
and he is afraid that the sympathetic bonds
which unite his artificial society would fail to
stand the strain of such an effort. He is content with a more modest and negative achievement; he will put a stop to the struggle for existence, but he will leave the struggle for the means
of existence still to rage. He hopes that the
struggle for the means of existence will elicit
the best; and in this hope, and for this end, he
seeks to secure the *carrière ouverte aux talents*,
by which the good shall ascend to their due

place, and not only so, but the bad shall also
descend to their proper level.

It is thus absurd to speak of an " ethics of
evolution," since evolution is a natural and
non-ethical process : we must invert the
phrase, and speak of an evolution of ethics.
Here, indeed, we may see a difficulty of the
same kind that confronts us in Hobbes.   How
can " natural man " evolve his " unnatural "
world of ethics ?   We seem to need some *deus
ex machina ;* and Dr. Russel Wallace, feeling
this need, has been driven to suppose some
" influx " from " the unseen universe of spirit "
to solve the difficulty. Huxley meets the
difficulty in a simpler way.   The self-restraint
of the moral world springs from organic factors
in the natural man.   The difficulty of this
answer is that it contradicts the antithesis of
the natural man and the social man which has
been so vividly emphasised; and here, indeed,
is the weakness of Huxley's whole position.
But let us set the difficulty aside, and follow
the argument. According to Huxley, the
organic factors of the natural man which
create society are two—family affection and,
more important still, the human instinct for
mimicry.   Like Bagehot and Tarde, Huxley
is an " imitationist."   We tend to imitate our
fellows : we want to be like our fellows : we
want to have the approval of our fellows.
This purely reflex operation of the mind, by
which, chameleon-like, we take the hue of
others, is the foundation of society.   Here
Huxley, it will be seen, is attempting a psychological explanation of the State.   The value
of such an explanation must be discussed

later; but in any case it is not obvious how an imitative aggregate can constitute a new moral world. In reality the problem of the existence of such a world, if we start from a basis like that of Huxley, is practically insoluble. It is difficult to see how imitative sympathy can produce an organised community directed to the good of mankind, or how imitative man can be anything of a magnificent rebel against nature. On such a system we are forced, after all, to take the State and its aims on trust, and to leave an unsolved dualism at the root of all our thought. Dualism, indeed, must always be the result, as long as we divide man with a hatchet into a self-asserting natural organism and a self-renouncing social being. The State will remain an unexplained negation of the natural man, the realm of an unexplained " do not," in which the individual loses himself, and outside which alone he can assert himself. It is only when we start from man as a whole; only when we conceive him as being, in his entirety, a rational being whose reason directs him to a good common to himself and other rational beings, that we can escape dualism, and find in the State a positive sphere of self-realisation in the attainment by common effort of a common good.

Huxley thus leaves the *raison d'être* of the State unexplained; and its function—the good of mankind—remains a mere assumption. Because the nature of the State is not made clear, its powers are left unlimited and indefinite. *Solvitur ambulando*, Huxley retorts; we can follow the empiric clue, and hold that

E 2

government may do anything which at any
given time will promote " the good of mankind." Natural rights avail nothing against
government; they constitute no limitation of
its powers; let government do what it can to
ensure the rule of peace in the cultivated
garden of the social world which has been
reclaimed from the wilderness of nature.
Now the things that belong to peace are civil
and moral rights; and to these rights duties
are attached (whereas no duties are attached
to natural rights); and the violation of these
duties must be punished. So we enter the
realm of " civil " freedom, where civil and
moral rights are guaranteed. To give such a
guarantee is the function of government.
But the guarantee is only given in the interests
of social peace, and it is only given in so far
as it is consistent with those interests. Those
interests are supreme. The State must obviously protect the interests of social peace by
war, and such protection must involve consequential " interference " with the liberty of
its members, to which no hard and fast limit
can be set, but which must vary with the
nature of each case. Thus, in the essay on
Administrative Nihilism, Huxley is led to defend
compulsory education on the ground of its
necessity for the promotion of social peace.
Here he runs counter to one of Spencer's doctrines; and though he is tender to Spencer
personally, he proceeds to attack the general
anarchist doctrine which Spencer had taught.
He denies that the State is a worse bungler
than any other " joint-stock company "; and
he urges that the analogy of the social organism

really favours the despotism of some " brain-centre." In the essay on *Government* he directs against Auberon Herbert's cult of " individual liberty " a fire of criticism which really riddles Spencer's position; for Herbert, in objecting to State-sanitation and State-education, in restricting the State to civil and criminal justice, and in conceiving all government as in its nature a usurpation, is exactly at one with Spencer. In all this polemic Huxley's attitude is not unlike that of Hobbes towards the Puritan individualists of his day; and indeed his kinship with Hobbes is obvious in many ways. But while Hobbes has something of the doctrinaire logic of Spencer, and while his logic makes him as extreme a partisan of government as Spencer was of anarchy, Huxley's strong common sense and lively sense of reality prevent him from being an apostle either of government or of anarchy. If he will not conceive the State as an anarchic society, because an anarchic society is a contradiction in terms, he will not conceive it as a social organism, because a social organism is also a contradiction in terms. A society, he urges, is not an organism; it is an artificial structure which implies, like every association, a basis of implied contract. Now contract involves two elements, an element of attraction —otherwise there would be no contract; and an element of repulsion—otherwise there would be not contract, but fusion. In man these two elements are the social inclination and the " unsocial peculiarity " of self-assertion. Since society has these two factors at its roots, government must be adjusted to both, and must recognise " two opposing tendencies of equal importance—the one restraining, the other encouraging, individual freedom." It must somehow balance the two empirically, and strike such a mean as the conditions of the hour and the public opinion of the day admit or demand.

A certain dualism, and with it a certain pessimism, remain as the conclusion of the whole matter. Huxley is not clear about self-assertion : sometimes it seems to be a moral attribute, sometimes the natural attribute of the ancient savage. On the whole, it tends to remain the latter. It is the element within us that binds us to the tumultuous process of cosmic nature. As such it bids us multiply in excess. Propagation is one of Nature's rules, for it is a necessary condition of that struggle which is her " law " ; but propagation brings us face to face with the " problem of problems," over-population, the insoluble Sphinx whose riddle we must solve on pain of death, and nevertheless can never solve. There is thus no happiness reserved for man, but rather " a constant struggle to maintain and improve, in opposition to the State of Nature, the State of Art of an organised polity." Our inheritance from our ancestors, our dose of original sin, is the " instinct of unlimited self-assertion "; we have the painful lesson of learning self-restraint and self-renunciation. Positive self-assertion, in Huxley as in Spencer, seems to be the mark of the animal; and both believe that so far as we are men, and members of a society which we have built as men, we are bound by a morality which is entirely negative.

Such a philosophy can hardly stand. We can
only justify ourselves, and we can only justify
the State which is part of ourselves and *is*
ourselves, if, in some such way as Green and
Bosanquet suggest, we believe that the self
and its individuality are asserted in and through
society, and that morality is something affirm-
ative, something in which we affirm our whole
selves, and not something in which we deny one
half of our nature.

Mr. Kidd, in *Social Evolution* (1894), follows the same path as Huxley, but seeks the
reconciliation of a dualistic world in and
through religion. The biologist, Mr. Kidd tells
us, must face and explain the phenomena of
group-life presented by human societies in the
same way and on the same principles as those
on which he deals with the simpler phenomena
of life. He must recognise the same fundamental law of natural selection—a law which
involves over-multiplication as its necessary
condition; which operates in the struggle for
survival among a surplus population; and
results in the refinement of the group-life
of society through the elimination of its
poorest and the selection of its strongest
elements. The law of life is a law which works
for the benefit of the " social organism," and
uses the " individual " as a mere means to its
ends. But the individual does not resign himself to the sacrifice without a struggle. The
reason which is in him, and which makes him
the individual that he is, rebels. Reason bids
him live for himself, assert himself, enjoy himself : " what are organisms to me," cries Reason,
" or I to them ? " But the law of life is after all

triumphant over insurgent reason. The law of life has an ally. That ally is Religion; and the law of life with the aid of Religion has through the ages defeated Reason. " Religion is a form of belief, providing an ultra-rational sanction for that large class of conduct in the individual where his interests and the interests of the social organism are antagonistic."

A curious obscurantism is thus the doctrine of Mr. Kidd. While Huxley regarded society as the product of a human reason that could fling a challenge in the face of Nature, Kidd regards societies or social organisms as the products of a law of life that overrides a recalcitrant but selfish reason, and enlists in its service, to secure its victory, a religion which apparently has nothing to do with reason, except, indeed, to keep it in subjection. So it follows that the evolutionary force of modern society is not intellect (intellect is rather a reactionary force tending to dislocate society), but the immense fund of religious sentiment generated by Christianity. " The evolution of human society is not primarily intellectual, but religious " : " there is only one way in which the rationalistic factor in human evolution can be controlled; namely, through the instrumentality of religious systems."

It is unnecessary to criticise Mr. Kidd. His conception of human reason, and his view of the relations between " individuals " and " social organisms," are curiosities rather than contributions to thought. On the other hand, a comparison of *Social Evolution* with Buckle's *History of Civilisation*, a work in some respects similar, written at the time of the Crimean

War, throws real light on the subsequent development of political thought under Darwinian
influence in the latter part of the nineteenth
century. Buckle, writing before the *Origin of
Species*, was concerned to make the science of
human society as stable and as certain as the
physical sciences. Both classes of science, he
felt, had to undertake the collection, collation
and interpretation of similar data in similar
ways. Buckle is thus scientific in a physico-
mathematical way, and what he borrows from
Science is rather method than content. By the
use of this method he is led to urge the influence
of physical factors like climate, soil and food
on the production and distribution of wealth.
He argues, for instance, that in hot climates
but little food is needed; that where little food
is needed, population multiplies rapidly; and
that where population multiplies rapidly, the
distribution of wealth is necessarily unfavour-
able to the labourer, and his wages are inevitably low. Something of the same easy
materialism also marks his discussion of the
production and distribution of thought. It is
a matter, he urges, of the " general aspect of
nature "; if Nature is too grand, thought is
stifled, and a wild imagination runs into super-
stition; if Nature is chary of her terrors, man
is confident and dares to think. If once he
can think, man has won the battle. It is
his thought which is the mainspring of
progress. The great truths of morals never
vary; their aspect is stationary. The truths
of the intellect are progressive; and it is these
progressive truths of intellect, and not the
stationary truths of morals, which alone can

explain progress.   Persecution has disappeared
not through the growth of humanity, but
through the growth of knowledge.   War tends
the more to disappear, the more gunpowder
liberates thought, by confining war to a professional class;   the more a knowledge of
political economy destroys the doctrines of
commercial enmity; the more the use of steam
gives men a greater acquaintance one with
another.   His belief in knowledge leads Buckle
to a disbelief in government.   It is not
governments, he argues, which produce the
progress of civilisation; it is knowledge.   He
even thinks that government is the enemy
of knowledge and therefore of progress.   It
took long years to inoculate the English Government with the new knowledge of political
economy taught by Adam Smith.   And when
government is finally induced to do something, what it does is not the creation of something new, but the undoing of something old.
We may be grateful for the removal of the
nuisance,.but why did the Government ever
put it there?   Government is a mere blun-
derer; " with the exception of certain necessary enactments respecting the preservation
of order . . . nearly everything which has
been done, has been done amiss."   The only
service a government can render to civilisation
is to keep order, and thereby to give an opportunity for the free knowledge of the individual
to produce, what it alone can produce, the
progress of the race.   Otherwise, one main
condition of the prosperity of a nation is that
its government should have but little power,
and should not use that little much.

The affinities of Buckle with Spencer, alike in his application of science to society, and in his contempt for the legislature, are obvious. It was the age of the Crystal Palace, when the waters were clear as glass, the individual knew himself, and the world trusted to his knowledge for its own proper going. The waters had been troubled when Kidd wrote. Knowledge did not seem so easy or so clear : Nature had been discovered to be as careless of the individual as she was careful of the type. The old harmony was gone; and a new harmony could only be attained, in Kidd's view, by setting up the type, or social organism, as final, and reconciling the individual to the type by giving the type the consecration of an unexplained religion.[1]

Hitherto we have seen science seeking to regard human activity as part of the process of cosmic nature, though we have found Huxley emphasising human rebellion against cosmic law, and Kidd recognising such rebellion, but administering an opiate of religion to the rebellious spirit. The spiritual element of humanity is either not recognised or, if it is recognised, it is treated as a mysterious exception to the natural law of the physical world. A very different application of scientific doctrine to human affairs appears in Leslie Stephen's *Science of Ethics* (1882) and

[1] The germ of Kidd's view may perhaps be detected in W. K. Clifford's essays on the "Scientific Basis of Morals" and on "Right and Wrong" (in his *Lectures and Essays*, ii. 106–107). These two essays, of the year 1875, represent early attempts to attain evolutionary ethics, and are admirable instances of Clifford's philosophic grasp and originality of view.

Prof. Alexander's *Moral Order and Progress* (1889). To them the human spirit is a central fact, which science cannot afford either to neglect or to banish into the limbo of mysterious exceptions, but is bound to explain. And thus, instead of seeing man imported as a physical substance into a physical world in the throes of natural evolution, we are taught to see evolution at work as a spiritual process in the spiritual world of human will. The spirit of man, it is argued by Walter Bagehot and Prof. Alexander, is subject to a spiritual evolution of its own—an evolution which takes the form of struggle between competing moral ideals, and issues in the survival of the fittest of such ideals.

Evolutionary ethics of this type, as expounded by Sir Leslie Stephen and Prof. Alexander, and also by Prof. Ritchie (in *Darwinism and Politics*, 1895) involves no application of supposed biological doctrines of laissez-faire and the right of might to the ethical world. Such application is indeed only too common. Darwinism has been pressed into political service by very different parties. Militarists have appealed to the ideas of struggle for existence and selection of the fittest in order to justify the selective agency of war. Individualists have appealed to the same ideas in order to find justification for an internal policy of laissez-faire, which shall not interfere with the selective activity of " beneficent struggle." It is in truth an easy procedure to steal Darwin's theory of the natural world and to apply it, without remembering *mutare mutanda*, to the spiritual world of human relations. It is easy to argue " Nature sets

her children to compete; let the State set its
citizens to do the like : Nature recognises the
strongest species as the right species; let the
human world recognise the strongest nation as
the right nation." But the essential feature
of the animal world is that it is unconscious :
the essential feature of the human world is that
it is conscious. The best can only be got out
of an unconscious animal world through physical
struggle, and at the cost of a tremendous waste
of life exterminated in the struggle; but it is
a huge and untenable assumption that the best
can only be got out of a conscious human world
by the same method, at the same cost. Man
would be a traitor to his humanity if he did
not seek to use his consciousness to get the best
out of himself without a physical struggle
which means waste. His struggle must be
peculiar, because he is peculiar : it must be
in the realm of consciousness, because he is
conscious; it must be self-determined, because
he is self-determining. We must beware at
any cost of that cheap fatalism, which issues
in the false doctrine of the predestination of
man by matter, and of election unto salvation by a mysterious environment. If we
replace this naturalistic travesty of Calvinism
by a belief in self-determining mind, then,
but not till then, we may apply doctrines of
evolution to human development. In such application we may either, with Prof. Alexander,
isolate the development of moral consciousness
for inquiry, and trace the analogy and identity
of the laws of this spiritual world with those
of the natural world; or we may, like Prof.
Hobhouse in *Democracy and Reaction* (1894),

urge that we are concerned with " orthogenic "
evolution, " consisting in the expansion of
mind," and we can trace this expansion from
the animals up to man, and from man to its
culmination " in the ideal of a collective
humanity, self-determining in its progress."
In either way we escape from materialism,
whether we do so, like Alexander, by emphasising the independence of the separate
process of spiritual evolution, or, like Hobhouse, by an insistence on the spirit of man
as the final product of natural evolution.   In
either way we find evolution used to support
the absolute predominance of spiritual right,
and not of material might, not only within
each state, but also in the relations of each
state with its fellows.   In either way we are
led to consider the conduct of men in societies
as primarily a matter of ethics.   And yet,
when all is said, it may still remain a matter
of doubt whether ethics and politics, which
belong to the sphere of mind, will gain by the
importation into their sphere, in whatever
way, of the laws of the natural world.

We turn to psychology.   Here again we
find an insistence on mind; and whatever
criticism one may pass on the application of
psychology to the philosophy of the State, such
application has this merit, that it does at any
rate proceed on the assumption that the State
is a product of mind, and must be interpreted
in terms of mind and not of Protozoa.   The
application of the psychological clue to the
riddles of human activity has indeed become
the fashion of the day.   If our fathers thought
biologically, we think psychologically.   Ever

since Jevons plunged into the mind of the consumer, and constructed the theory of final value, economists have tended to be more and more psychological. Ever since Bagehot wrote *Physics and Politics*, political theorists have turned social psychologists; they have approached the facts of group-life on the assumption that these facts are facts of group-consciousness, which it is their problem to describe and explain by means of the method which a natural science uses in order to describe and explain the facts of matter. Accordingly, just as the psychologist regards himself as studying, by means of the methods of natural science, a subject-matter consisting in " states of consciousness as such," so the social psychologist regards himself as studying, by means of the same methods, a subject-matter consisting in states of group-consciousness as such. It is important to notice that social psychology, using the methods of natural science, regards itself as a branch of natural science. Two results follow from this point of view. In the first place, it follows that social psychology must study all the data of group-consciousness —not only the later and more complex, but also the simple and the primitive as they appear among animals and in early human societies; and it also follows, as a result, that social psychology must tend, like a natural science such as chemistry, to seek to resolve the complex into terms of the primitive. In the second place, it follows on its being a branch of natural science, that all the data of social psychology are of equal value to the social psychologist. Nitrogen is no more valuable

than oxygen to the chemist; and the totem is
no less valuable than the trades union to the
social psychologist. He does not deal in terms
of value. Values belong to the moralist. This
means that the psychologist, after all, does not
greatly transcend the biologist when he turns
his attention to politics. Both are fundamentally alike in following the procedure of
natural science. So far as the one or the other
speaks in terms of value, he is transcending his
limits as a student of natural science, and turning a moralist. The advantage of the psychologist lies in the fact that, just because he is
studying mind, he is constantly driven to
transcend his limits to a greater extent than
the biologist. He has a greater tendency to
grade and to value the different facts of consciousness and group-consciousness. It is his
disadvantage that he tends to grade such facts
from the wrong end; to make the beginning
prior not only in time but in importance to the
end; in a word, to explain civilised life in
terms of savage instinct. It is his disadvantage, again, that engaged in the study of
" states of consciousness," he is necessarily
driven back on the isolated sentience of the
individual mind which has this consciousness.
The world becomes a sum of such isolated sen-
tiences; and in order to combine them, and
thus to attain to " states of group-consciousness," he invokes some primary factor in their
sentience like imitation. This is to explain
society as an irrational structure, and therefore
not to explain society at all. Social psychology
leads us first into the materialism of explaining
the higher by the lower, and then into the

irrationalism of seeing in society the result of imitation, and in its citizens the hypnotised product of arbitrary suggestion.

Though Bagehot gives to his book the title *Physics and Politics* (1873), and the subtitle of " thoughts on the application of the principles of natural selection and inheritance to political society," his book is concerned with " psychics " and not with physics, and his thoughts are chiefly about the application of the principle of imitation to politics. His book is really the beginning of the psychological method : it is a fine imaginative recapture of prehistory by the use of psychological analogy. His contention is that an early society has to form a large area of reflex action—a cake of custom—in order to attain any solidity, just as a later society has to break away from this area in order to attain any progress. His explanation of both processes is fundamentally psychological. It is true that at times he tends to ascribe the perpetuation of custom to a cause now discredited—the " inheritance " of acquired faculties; it is true that the " natural selection " of early war is pressed into service in order to explain why early societies must, on peril of their lives, form and preserve their custom. But much the larger and more valuable element of his book is its brilliant psychological aperçus; and as a matter of fact he really ascribes the formation and the perpetuation of custom to the psychological force of imitation. Bagehot was a Tardian years before Tarde wrote *Les Lois de l'Imitation*. He uses analogies drawn equally from the style of the leaders of the *Times* and

the habits of boarding schools to show how
a style or type of character which has gained a
" chance-predominance " is unconsciously imi-
tated, while its opposites are correspondingly
persecuted, until it becomes the general habit
or hereditary drill of a society. Imitation is
always the moulding force, if a desire for success in war is generally the driving motive, of
early customary societies. Men have to imitate the successful type in order to be successful,
but they will imitate it anyhow. The great
difficulty, indeed, is to stop imitation, and so
to make progress possible. Here Bagehot
introduces a new psychological force—the
instinct for discussion; and in explaining this
force he makes some of his finest and most
penetrating suggestions. Imitation is universal; discussion is the prerogative of a
few societies; and this is the reason why
progress is confined to a small area of the
world. Discussion does much for the societies
in which it is engrained. It means that for
these societies nothing is true because it
is customary, or right because it exists; it
means that a habit of toleration of opinion is
developed; it means that the mere barbarous
impulse to " do something " is checked, and
that men, " looking "—and talking—" before
they leap," leap less and so fare better. In
this way Bagehot comes to draw a distinction,
almost reminiscent of Spencer, between the
military age—with its stern customary regimentation, and at the same time its impulse
to hasty action—and the age of discussion, with
its quiet toleration of opinion, its postponement
of action, and its preference for thought.

The application of psychology to politics since the days of Bagehot has been chiefly characteristic of French writers—Tarde, the most prominent; Durkheim, perhaps the most profound; Le Bon, the most popular, and the most superficial. In England two recent writers have attempted this application— Graham Wallas, in his *Human Nature in Politics* (1908), and MacDougall, in his *Social Psychology* (1908). Mr. Graham Wallas seems to smile, with a sort of very kindly pessimism, at the psychological foundations of modern societies. " Away with the intellectualist fallacy," is his first warning : " politics is only in a slight degree the product of conscious reason : it is largely a matter of subconscious processes of habit and instinct, suggestion and imitation." In other words, we must enter by the back-door : the front-door is very seldom open. Mr. Graham Wallas therefore takes his start from a sensationalist philosophy, though he manages, unlike sensationalists such as Hume, to avoid a political philosophy of absolutism. " Man, *like other animals*, lives in an unending stream of sense impressions." This sensationalism is combined with a nominalism like that of the later scholastics, who, as Harnack says, " had also discovered the importance of the concrete as compared with hollow abstractions, and to their perception of this gave brilliant expression, *e. g.* in psychology." From the unending stream of sense impressions we seize for emphasis that which, when it occurs, is like something previous to itself; provided, indeed, that it is also significant, or. in other words, that it suggests a *set* of im-

pressions of which it is the clue or key. Hence
arise the names (or *nomina*) which indicate
likeness and have also significance, such as the
names of parties, Liberal and Conservative;
hence also arise symbols, which are visible
rather than audible, and appeal to that
majority which is " visualist " rather than
" audile," such as the party colours, red and
blue. These names or symbols may have
intellectualist origins; " justice," as formulated
by Socrates, had that origin. They may also,
when they have become current, suggest to
intellectuals ideas of an intellectual order;
" my country " may mean to the philosopher a
rational conception of a living social organism.
But what they suggest to the mass of us, and
suggest automatically, is an emotion, in the
sense of a set of impressions habitually associated with the name. " Country " and
" party " are such names; and institutions are
thus not so much ideas, as emotion-charged
and emotion-evoking names. Here enters the
art of the politician. He makes names, as
Mazzini made the magic name " Italia "; and
he can play on the suggestibility of the mass
till he makes the name a great emotional symbol.
Here we reach the psychological substratum of
modern elections. They are, or tend to be,
psychological orgies : they are exercises in
" spell-binding "; the party names and symbols,
the party colours, placards and songs are all
let loose on the suggestibility of the electorate.

The same theory of " suggestion," which
Mr. Graham Wallas applies to politics, has
been applied to education; and the teacher has
been conceived as suggesting, consciously or

unconsciously, intellectual and moral lessons
to his pupils. It has also been applied to
economics : the advertiser may be regarded, in
something the same way as the teacher, as
suggesting, though in a highly conscious
manner, exaggerated values for the wares
which he advertises under a magic name. A
close analogy may indeed be drawn between
the advertisement of political values under
magic names or symbols, and the advertisement of economic values. "The empirical
art of politics consists largely in the creation of
opinion by the deliberate exploitation of subconscious non-rational inference." If this be
so, the question obviously rises, whether there
is any reason or hope for democracy or representation. Why should we not simply leave
the best intellects to play on the suggestibility
of the mass as best they can? Because,
Mr. Graham Wallas replies, the best intellects
are themselves the prey of suggestion; because
" government without consent is a complicated
and ugly process "; above all, because more
stringent electoral laws, and a greater spread
of education, may produce more sweetness and
light. Moreover, good may somehow come
out of all this suggestiveness of names; and
Mr. Wallas devotes a final chapter to speculation about a time when the name of Humanity
may become charged with emotion, and " an
idea of the whole existence of our species " may
prove to have not less emotional effect than
" that of the visible temples and walls of the
Greek cities."

This is a brief, and perhaps, in both senses of
the word, a too partial sketch of a book which

is itself eminently " suggestive." Many lines of criticism occur. Something could be said of its sensationalist premisses; something of its nominalist philosophy; something of that tendency to explain the higher in terms of the lower, which leads to the explanation of civilised life by the conditions of life in pre-historic times and to the repeated coupling of man with " the other animals." We might urge that reason is none the less reason when it is not conscious inference, and that it is a fallacy to derationalise political society because it is not an explicit organisation of conscious reason. Better however than to criticise is to emphasise the truths which Mr. Graham Wallas suggests. In the first place, he has analysed that automatic area of reflex action—habit and instinct, suggestion and imitation—which does exist and does need its analysis, though it exists, as we have seen before, in conjunction with, or rather in the service of, an intelligence which -does not lose its freedom, but rather secures that freshness which is necessary to its freedom, through such conjunction and service. He has shown that this automatic area has its dangers, as well as its uses—that it may defeat, unless it is carefully controlled, the intelligence which it serves. He has suggested that, if we are to understand the fulness of the operation of mind, we must not make it a merely mechanical principle; we must not reduce it, with the Benthamites, to a calculating machine, proceeding, in the same way for all men, on the one standard of pleasures and pains. We must see mind in its fulness in the " human type "; we must see it in its diversity in the multitudinous variations from the type; and for this purpose we must employ the quantitative method of statistics. On this last point, indeed, it may be argued that Mr. Graham Wallas is running out of political theory into the political art of the practical statesman, and that theory studies the " pure " instance, if practice has to reckon with variations.

But at any rate the fulness of the type does need recognition; and this is the point which Mr. MacDougall also enforces in *Social Psychology.* Broadening the definition of psychology, and making it not a static science of states of consciousness, but a dynamic science of conduct or behaviour, which deals with the issue of consciousness in action, he too would urge that political theory, just like economic theory, needs the aid of psychology if it is to have a conception of mind and its operations full and real enough to make it fruitful. The difficulty is, when it comes to the point, that Mr. MacDougall, while giving a full account of the genesis of instincts that act *in* society, hardly shows how thay issue *into* society. He seems to do a great deal of packing in preparation for a journey on which he never starts. The " intellectualists " may not do enough packing, but at any rate they do travel into and even explore the state.

Social psychology leads us to sociology. Sociology, roughly speaking, attempts a synthesis of biology and social psychology, though it also runs into other studies like anthropology, and even jurisprudence and economics. Indeed it is a Napoleonic study : it seeks to incorporate in its empire the whole continent of the

social sciences. Comte was the father of the
name; and the significance he sought to attach
to the name was that of the " positive "
study (positive in the sense of being divorced
from theological or metaphysical assumptions)
of " social physics "—that is to say, of the
natural causes and natural laws of society.
Spencer was the next to use the word and
study the subject. Starting like Comte from
a conception of sociology as a species of social
physics or " statics," he advanced to a later
view which made it a matter of social biology,
and beyond that again to a still later view,
which turned sociology into the study of
social psychology. But on the whole we may
say, with Prof. Giddings, that " Spencerian
Sociology . . . is to a large extent a physical
philosophy of society, notwithstanding its
liberal use of biological and psychological
data." It has thus a Comtist character, but
it differs from Comtism on some essential
points. Its practical outcome is not the scientific regulation of society, but the exact opposite
of such regulation. Just because there are
laws, and because these laws may be trusted
to operate, Spencer thinks that the statesman
had better leave well alone. Again Comte
had regarded sociology as the one and only
science of human action. Believing the life
of society to be an organically interdependent
whole, he had banished would-be special or
departmental sciences like political economy.
Spencer is willing to treat sociology as a co-
ordinating science, and to leave room for the
separate sciences which it co-ordinates. It is
a synthesis within the great synthetic philo-

sophy : it is the particular application of the universal truth of evolution to a great department of co-ordinated sciences, which forms a single subject of study in virtue of being amenable to this application.

According to Prof. Giddings (*Sociology*, 1896), whom we may take as a representative of modern sociology, the science must emphasise the subjective as well as the objective side of the constitution of man. It must study social volition as well as physical evolution; it must embrace social psychology as well as social biology. The weakness of the science, Prof. Giddings feels, lies in the department of psychology. Biology does supply a principle to sociology—the principle of evolution. Psychology has tended to supply nothing more than a tiresome enumeration of all the motives that actuate man in his social relations. What is needed is a principle; and Prof. Giddings, following but extending the generalisations of Tarde, finds the original and elementary subjective fact in "consciousness of kind." Sociology has thus to trace and to relate to one another the operations of the two principles of evolution and of consciousness of kind in human societies. It takes those parts of the sciences of biology and of psychology which relate to societies of men; and it constitutes itself into a science by correlating these data with the facts of human society. Thus conceived it is broader than political theory, which is only one of its departments. Political theory only deals with political associations, united by a constitution and living under a government : sociology deals with all association.

Political theory assumes as a datum that **man** *is* a political being; it does not explain, as sociology seeks to do, how he came to be a political being.

A political theorist might seek to invert this relation. He might claim that it is the highest and most typical association which he isolates for study, and that in doing so he never forgets its relation to other associations; he might urge that, if sociologists are concerned with genesis, he is concerned with the deeper problems of *raison d'être* and value. But there is no need to quarrel about names and the boundaries of studies, if sociology produces good fruits. And this it seems likely to do, if it follows the lines on which it seems to be moving. The sociologist will start from habits, instincts, emotions, but at any rate he will end in a conception of association as based on intelligent reason. The political theorist starts at the opposite end with rational association; but he admits that there exists, and must be taken into account, a sub-rational area of instinct. The difference between the two methods is not profound.

NOTE.—Space has not permitted any examination of the new branch of studies called Eugenics. On this subject, and indeed on the relation of biology to politics in general, the reader should consult the thirty compact pages of Mr. Bateson's pamphlet, *Biological Fact and the Structure of Society*. Particularly important are the pages (24–34) in which Mr. Bateson, adopting the biological conception of a social organism, discusses its bearing on the ideals of socialism and democracy. He argues that the conception demands a society articulated in permanent classes, each content with its function. This view has its affinities with the teaching of Plato, and also, as Mr. Bateson shows, with

the mediæval idea of a system of " Estates." It issues
in a criticism of democracy and in a comparatively
favourable attitude to socialism—ideals which are argued
to be incompatible. On the other hand, Mr. Bateson also
criticises socialism, on the ground that it would be adverse
to the emergence of those exceptional variations, or
"mutational novelties," which are necessary to the
progress of society.

CHAPTER VI

THE LAWYERS

In 1859 appeared Darwin's *Origin of Species*;
in 1861 was published Sir Henry Maine's
Ancient Law. We need not suspect more
than concomitance; but the concomitance
between Darwin's application of history to
biology, and Maine's application of history
to law, is at any rate to be noted. Maine saw
the connection, and in later years he hastened
to borrow new weapons from the armoury of
Darwin. In *Early Law and Custom* he cites
Darwin in support of the patriarchal theory of
the origin of early society. In *Popular Government* he makes it part of his indictment against
democracy, that the multitude evidently dis-
likes the doctrine of the struggle for existence
—" that beneficent private war," he writes,
" which makes one man strive to climb on the
shoulders of another and remain there through
the law of the survival of the fittest." Finally,
his feeling for aristocracies, and for the English
Second Chamber in particular, depends on a
belief, whether Darwinian or Lamarckian, in
the hereditary transmission of mental qualities.

F

Maine's Historical Method has, however, a definite ancestry of its own in its own sphere. Without forgetting the pioneer work done by Montesquieu in the *Esprit des Lois* (1748), we may say that the method is the child of the French Revolution—a child, as children sometimes are, in strong reaction against the ways of its parent. On the revolutionary assertion of natural rights, and the revolutionary belief in an ideal system of society which was everywhere and always valid, there was bound to follow, in the natural development of thought, an assertion of the place of rooted and ingrained custom and a belief in the doctrines of environment and relativity. Rather as a spirit than as a method, this tendency already appears in the splendid romanticism of Burke. It inspires the romantic literature of the Continent : it breathes in the movement of politics after 1815. In France it lies behind the Catholic exaltation and mediæval fervour of Chateaubriand and Montalembert, De Maistre and Lamennais; and it comes to light in curious ways in the teaching both of St. Simon, at once a mediævalist and a Utopian, and of Auguste Comte, in early years the disciple of St. Simon, and in later years still imbued with the traces of his discipleship. Even his own peculiar gospel of Positivism, unromantic as it may seem, carried Comte forward to a cult of history. If we must banish theological and metaphysical pre-suppositions, and if we must take things as they are, it follows that we must banish natural rights and that we must take history as we find it. We must accept each complex of historical facts; we must explain each complex, in the sense of bringing it within the sphere of regularity or scientific law, by referring it to the series of its antecedents, and by eliciting it from the conditions inherent in its own particular stage of social existence. In this process we shall necessarily give due weight to relativity and environment: we shall recognise, in other words, that each social stage is as perfect as the conditions and the environment whose product it is will permit it to be. This is a line of thought which Mill himself, whether under the influence of Comte or that of Coleridge, was also prepared to tread. The fundamental problem of the general science of society is, he writes in his *Logic,* "to find the laws according to which any state of Society produces the State which succeeds it and takes its place." [1]

But it is from Germany that the Historical Method, as it appears in Maine, derives its greatest inspiration. From the beginning of the nineteenth century that method had definitely begun to be used in Germany, and it had been used in the very same sphere of law in which it was afterwards used by Maine. While in France the historical spirit had been allied with reaction, and while its motto had been " Back to the Middle Ages " (a motto ever recurrent in very diverse forms, to-day in the form of devout Ultramontanism, to-morrow in

[1] Comte's view that the industrial régime supersedes the military, as "positive" thought supersedes metaphysical, is one of importance. As it is perhaps drawn from St. Simon, so it seems to influence, and at any rate it resembles, the antithesis drawn by Spencer between industrial and military society, and that drawn by Maine between contract and status.

the form of Guild-Socialism), in Germany that
spirit had been allied with patriotism, and its
motto had been " The Historical Nation and
its Historical Law." Eichhorn set the fashion
of the historical treatment of law; Savigny
carried his teaching forward. " Law," he told
the world, " is the organ of folk-right : it moves
and grows like every other expression of the
life of the people : it is formed by custom
and popular feeling, through the operation of
silent forces, and not by the arbitrary will of
a legislator."

Savigny, when he wrote in this sense, was
opposing the idea of a new German code.
Maine, when he wrote in a similar sense in
Ancient Law, was opposing at one and the same
time two schools, which were themselves opposed to one another—the school of Rousseau
and the school of Bentham. He had set his
lance against first principles, whether of
" general will " or of " greatest happiness ";
and abandoning any *a priori* assumption of the
final causes of human society, he was resolved
to pursue a realistic treatment of social phenomena in the light of the historical data of law.
He would analyse society in the terms of its
legal structure; he would use a method at once
historical, in the sense of being based on
chronological data arranged in a sequence of
development, and comparative, in the sense of
being based on an induction from the customs
of different peoples living in the same stage of
growth. The value of Maine's method lies in
his firm grip of the idea of evolution—in his
deep sense of the generations as

Linked each to each by natural piety.

If the doctrine of evolution, as Sir Frederic
Pollock has said, is nothing else than the historical method applied to the facts of nature,
the historical method, as he adds, is nothing
else than the doctrine of evolution applied to
human institutions. Such an application—if
it reinforces, as it should, the old lesson that
constitutions are like poets (*nascuntur, non
fiunt*); if it reiterates, as it should, the old
warning that the roots of the present lie deep
in the past—has its own proper justification.

It has also its own limitations. In the first
place, it is difficult to say that there is any one
line of human evolution. There are many
lines—some that suddenly stop, some that turn
back, some that cross one another; and one
may think rather of the maze of tracks on a
wide common than of any broad king's highway. Maine's own highway runs from Status
to Contract. Men start from positions inevitably determined by their membership of
the groups in which they find themselves : they
end in positions freely determined by contracts
to which they pledge themselves. Granted
that the process to contract seemed obvious in
1861, when competition and free contract ran
riot, it is by no means equally evident to-day.
Nor is the process from status, as conceived
by Maine, with his assumption that organised
society starts from the patriarchal family-
group, a process which we can readily assume
to have been universal. But even if historical
laws were exact, and even if they were universal, there is a limitation to their value,
which Maine does not always recognise. History cannot answer the riddles of the Sphinx.

It can trace a process; it cannot determine the value of the result. However sublimated it may be, it remains history. It remains a record of what was, and of how it came to be. It cannot attain to a view of what ought to be, or to an explanation of why it should be, though it can help such attainment by giving the philosopher a survey of human ideals and a sketch of the institutions in which men have sought to realise those ideals. If this be so, it follows that it is no answer to a philosophic explanation of the *raison d'être* and value of the State, such as the explanation of Rousseau, to urge that it is contradicted by history and the historic method. Maine does not disprove the doctrine of natural rights and social contract by alleging that " history shows " society beginning not with individual rights but with group-status, and not with free contract but with paternal power. " History shows " very little, if anything, about ultimate questions; and in any case the apostles of natural rights and social contract were not concerned with historical origins. They were thinking not of the chronological antecedents, but of the logical presuppositions, of political society. They meant that they could only explain society if they presupposed contracting individuals with individual rights, just as most of us would say that we can only explain the whole world of human life if we presuppose a God. The latter presupposition would not be invalidated, if historians amassed a thousand instances of primitive tribes which knew no God; the former presupposition is not invalidated by a thousand instances of primitive paternal power. It can only be invalidated by a proof either that it fails to explain what it has to explain, or that this can be explained otherwise; and such a proof, though it is possible, is not possible to history.

The final upshot of the Historical Method, if we turn to *Popular Government* (1885), seems to be a somewhat melancholy conservatism. " It is no mere accident," says Dicey, " that Maine, who in his *Ancient Law* undermined the authority of analytical jurisprudence, aimed in his *Popular Government* a blow at the foundations of Benthamite faith in democracy." History does not furnish Maine, as it furnished Acton, with any guiding thread of growing freedom; and the process towards contract does not appear in the issue to be a process towards liberty. What History proves is the rarity and fragility of democracy. History has with Maine, what it tends to have with many of us, a way of numbing generous emotions. All things have happened already; nothing much came of them before; and nothing much can be expected of them now. This frame of mind was encouraged by the fears engendered during the constitutional crisis of 1884, fears which impressed strongly on Maine's mind the need of some check on constitutional change. Perhaps, too, his experience and knowledge of India may have had some influence towards a conservative bias. It would indeed be an interesting problem to discover the effects of service in India, and the habit of mind induced by service in India, on the political speculation of the last fifty years. Sir James Stephen confesses, in the dedication of his *Liberty, Equality, Fraternity* (1873), that his " Indian experience strongly confirmed the reflections which the book contains." The influence of India on Maine seems equally patent.

The chief factor, however, in Maine's con-servatism, is perhaps at bottom the professional instinct of the lawyer. The lawyer does not readily welcome legal change by an inexpert legislature; he prefers the traditional wisdom of his own profession. This is the deepest reason for Maine's aversion to change, that masker in the guise of progress, and to democracy, "the form of government" most favourable, or at any rate assumed by its parti-sans to be most favourable, to change. The general argument of *Popular Government* pro-ceeds from a sort of intellectual anti-intel-lectualism. Assuming, like some French writers, such as Renan and afterwards Tarde, that aristocracy is the mother of all real pro-gress, and holding that the multitude has been the enemy of all fruitful novelty, Maine argues that democracy, whatever its love of change during its militant phase, will in its triumphant phase pass into a Chinese stationary State. But he does not really anticipate its triumph. Democracy is only a "form of government" (its partisans would reply that it is no form of government at all, but a mode of the spirit, an attitude of mind ineradicable when once at-tained); and it is a form which must be judged by the efficiency of its results (to which its partisans would again reply, that it is not the efficiency of its "results," but the energy of the spirit itself, which is the criterion of any mode of the spirit, whether in education or in politics). Judged by its results, as they appear in his-

tory, democracy is fragile : judged by its
working, as we see it to-day, it is a form of
government which can only exist by the aid
of two evil methods—the organisation of party,
which entails corruption of the electorate either
singly or in classes, and the feeding of the
electoral mind on the empty husks of mere
generalities like Liberty and Equality.   Its end
is likely to be the exhaustion of the common
stock of good things, an exhaustion achieved
by mutiny and sedition under the plea of an
equitable re-division.   The one salvation for
" the Englishmen who now live *in fœce
Romuli* " is apparently the accumulation of
brakes to stop the rake's progress into the
abyss.   *Ex America lux ;* and Maine turns to
the United States, and urges the need of our
recognising, like the United States, that there
is a distinction between constitutional and legal
change, and that constitutional change needs
special solemnity and special sanction.   From
America he also learns another lesson.   He
learns the value of setting an historical principle
to serve as a check on pure democracy ; and
thus by the side of the Senate, which represents
that principle in the United States, he would
set, as its English representative, the House of
Lords, reformed perhaps in its composition,
but not too greatly reformed, and at any rate
unimpaired or even increased in its powers.

This is Maine's political philosophy, buttressed incidentally by a denunciation of
Rousseauism as historically baseless and viti-
ated by the fact that no communities ever
were formed in the way imagined by Rousseau.
In reality Maine, with his gift for massive and

impressive generalisation, was the tragic voice, sonorous behind the mask of Cassandra, which uttered the feelings that had gathered since the extension of the suffrage in 1867. Mill himself, eager for the representation of minorities, and anxious above all things for liberty of opinion, had helped to swell the voice of warning. Bagehot, sympathetic and profound as was his analysis of the *English Constitution* (1867), had been uneasy about the leap in the dark, and anxious for the education of the new masters of England. Cornewall Lewis, Liberal politician, and critic of the legends of early Roman History, had shown, in works like the *Essay on the Government of Dependencies* (1841), and the *Dialogue on the Best Form of Government* (1863), the sceptical attitude of a practical and critical intellect towards theories, and the belief, natural to an administrator, that "whate'er is best administered is best." Above all, Stephen's *Liberty, Equality, Fraternity* (1873), had served as a critique, no less trenchant than profound, of the democratic tendencies of the Utilitarian School. A lawyer, and the historian of English Criminal Law; a strong believer in the religious foundations of human life and action; a thinker influenced by his experiences of India, Stephen was led on every ground to pit the principle of Authority against the principle of Utility. Authority, in its human foundations, means the compulsion of the few over the many, whether such compulsion be exercised by force or by persuasion. Even parliamentary government is a disguised form of compulsion; "we agree to try strength by counting heads instead of breaking heads";

and such compulsion only grows with civilisation. " President Lincoln attained his objects by the use of a degree of force which would have crushed Charlemagne and his paladins and peers like so many egg-shells." Compulsion and force, however, have their own profound and ultimate foundations. All government must have a moral basis ; and the connection between morals and religion is in turn so intimate that this basis must in the final analysis be considered as religious. Refusing to distinguish between temporal and spiritual (for human life is one and indivisible), Stephen argues for the single and undivided control of life by a government resting on a religious basis. A government resting on such a basis will exercise compulsion, if and provided that it is satisfied, first, that the objects for which compulsion is exercised are generally, and on grounds which are ultimately religious, held to be good; secondly, that compulsion can attain those objects; and lastly, that it can attain them without too great an expense. Such compulsion will be exercised partly by the coercive force of law, both criminal and civil, and partly through the coercive influence of public opinion. The responsive quality of mind which every society demands and elicits from its members is therefore discipline—discipline in its widest sense; discipline as an astringent force giving to every human being his maximum of power. It is of discipline, whereby we are attuned to the deep compulsory truths of existence, rather than of progress or of liberty, that the wise politician will do well to think. Progress is a mixed thing, partly good and partly bad. One bad effect it has at any rate exercised; it has weakened the pristine strength of manhood. Nor is this all. Progress, as it marches " from status to contract," has helped to produce the glaring inequalities of fortune which free contract breeds. Liberty fares little better than progress in Stephen's philosophy. Liberty, which has no connection with the form of government called democracy, since that form may be intolerably compulsory, is a negation, a hole in a waterpipe; and it is far better to study the waters of human nature and to understand the deep springs of human action than to investigate the nature of holes. As for democracy, or universal suffrage, it is an institution calculated to secure general consent for whatever is done, and to interest a great many people in the transaction of human affairs, nor is there anything that can take its place; but the cost of such a system in point of efficiency is enormous, and the system only means, when all is said and done, the rule of the few manipulators who can collect suffrages in their own favour with the greatest success.

Stephen's book is the finest exposition of conservative thought in the latter half of the nineteenth century. It is a robust polemic, sometimes extravagant in its epigrams, but tinged throughout by that belief in the religious basis of human society which has been the strength of conservatism from Burke to to-day. It is a frank and die-hard statement of the ideas dominant among the educated and governing classes of English society. But Stephen's splendid single star did not make a constellation;

and while he influenced Maine, he did not exert Maine's influence. The influence of Maine, it is true, was not the influence of his conservative tenets, but rather that of his new methods. Those methods have much to do with the growth of two new subjects of study—comparative politics and anthropology. Seeley and Freeman, professors of history at Cambridge and Oxford, have both attempted a survey of political institutions on something of an historical and comparative method; and the *Introduction to Political Science* (1896) of the one, and the *Comparative Politics* (1873) of the other, are the somewhat jejune fruits of the attempt.[1] Anthropology, a study which owes much to Maine, has prospered far more largely. His attempt to reconstruct primitive society from legal evidence has stimulated, by way of imitation or reaction, a large number of scholars. The brothers McLennan attacked his conception of primitive society in their *Patriarchal Theory* (1885); and the writings of Robertson Smith (especially *The Religion of the Semites*, 1889), and of Westermarck (more especially *The History of Human Marriage*, 1891) have thrown new light on the problems first suggested by Maine.

It was from the study of early law that Maine sought to throw new light on politics : it is from the study of the constitution and the law of contemporary England that Prof. Dicey has sought to draw a fuller insight into the political principles which dominate English life.

[1] The most solid and valuable work in this field is that of Lord Bryce, whose *Studies in History and Jurisprudence*, in particular, are full of penetrating analysis and suggestive comparison.

In the *Law of the Constitution* (1885) he analyses the English Constitution, and by comparison with America and contrast with France he shows that one of its most fundamental principles is the "rule of law." Government in England has no arbitrary power; all men are subject in all things to the ordinary law administered by the ordinary courts; and that law contains the law of the constitution itself, which has no distinct or separate existence, but is a part, and indeed a result, of the ordinary law of the land. In these things England is distinct from France, with her separate system of *droit administratif;* and on the other hand, at any rate in one fundamental respect, she is cognate with America, which like England possesses no separate body of administrative law. As in the *Law of the Constitution* Dicey analyses the constitution of England to discover its fundamental principle, so in *Law and Opinion in England* (1905) he analyses the English legislation of the nineteenth century, in order to elucidate, by a comparison of its successive stages, the principles of politics and ethics by which it has been guided in each stage. He finds three such stages—the period of old Toryism, from 1800 to 1830; the period of Benthamism, from 1825 to 1870; and the period of " Collectivism," from 1865 to 1900. His method is analytical and not dogmatic; but so far as he has a dogma of his own to advance it is Benthamism. As a Benthamite, he hardly shares the distrust of democracy which Maine and Stephen both show. He urges that democracy is no uniform thing, producing uniform results in each State in which it is adopted. On the contrary, it varies in its effects from State to State, according to the national temperament of each State ; and in England the peculiar form of " democracy tempered by snobbishness " which is congenial to our national temperament has not unduly hastened change or greatly favoured " the party of progress."

Dicey's influence has largely gone towards showing us where we stand already, rather than towards guiding us in new directions. The influence which Prof. Maitland has exercised in late years has been more of the latter order. Stimulated by German speculations into the nature of groups and their proper legal position in the State, Maitland has in turn stimulated English students to pursue this line of inquiry. Under the influence of the great jurist Gierke, Maitland was led to embrace the doctrine of the " real personality " of the group. In his Introduction to *Political Theories of the Middle Age* (1900), and in a number of papers in the third volume of his *Collected Papers*, he has enunciated the doctrine and sought to elicit some of its lessons. More recently Dr. Figgis, particularly in *Churches in the Modern State* (1913), has advocated the same doctrine, and enlisted it in support of the rights of ecclesiastical groups.

The new doctrine runs somewhat as follows. No permanent group, permanently organised for a durable object, can be regarded as a mere sum of persons, whose union, to have any rights or duties, must receive a legal confirmation. Permanent groups are themselves persons, group-persons, with a group-will of their own and a permanent character of their own; and they have become group-persons of themselves, without any " creative " act of the State. In a word, group-persons are real persons; and just because they are so, and possess such attributes of persons as will and character, they cannot have been made by the State. No external power can make a real person : a real person grows from within. It is possible to have doubts about part of this doctrine, and yet to accept and to urge its main tenet. To talk of the real personality of anything, other than the individual human being, is to indulge in dubious and perhaps nebulous speech. When a permanent group of ninety-nine members is in session in its place of meeting, engaged in willing the policy of the group, it is permissible to doubt whether a hundredth person supervenes. The solution of the doubt would involve the determination of metaphysical questions beyond the scope of this argument. But we are entitled to assume that permanently organised groups are at any rate juristic personalities. They are capable, that is to say, of contracting obligations : they can sue and be sued. Such juristic personality is a different concept from real personality. Juristic personality is a source, not necessarily situate in a single being, of certain kinds of action of a legal nature, such as owning land, or suing in courts, or the like. Real personality is a single source of action in general, that is to say, of all kinds of action. A real person may not be a juristic person; women, for instance, for a long period in the history of Roman law were not juristic persons. On the other hand a juristic person, such as a permanent group, may conceivably not be a real person. But in any case, even if we reduce the group to the category of a juristic person, we may still hold to Maitland's main tenet, and plead that such personality grows and is not made. In other words, these juristic persons can exist, and do exist, before there is any legal act of incorporation or " creation," just as law itself can exist, and does exist, before there is any legal act of legislation. Law, Gierke writes, is the result of a common conviction not that a thing shall be, but that it is; and in the same way we may hold that juristic personality is the result of a common conviction not that corporate persons shall be allowed to exist, but that they exist already. And just as statute law is a recognition of something which already exists, so legal incorporation may also be recognition of something already in existence.

It is obvious that, if this position be accepted, the theory of the State is vitally affected. For one thing the mere emphasis laid on groups, whatever may be our ultimate theory of their origin, in itself affects our theory of the State. We see the State less as an association of individuals in a common life : we see it more as an association of individuals, already united in various groups each with its common life, in a further and higher group for a further and more embracing common purpose In the second place we shall not only give a new nuance to our general conception of the State; we shall also tend to alter our theory of the relations of the State and associations. If we hold that a juristic person is born of a common conviction, and that it may exist in and through a social recognition which treats an association as such a person apart from and prior to any legal act of " creation," we shall at once in one respect limit, and in others enfranchise, our associations. We shall limit them in the sense that we shall treat them as persons, subject to the liabilities of persons, whether or no there has been a legal act of creation. If juristic personality does not depend on creation, a juristic person may be liable to responsibilities without creation; and it cannot evade those responsibilities by pleading that it had not been made a person *de jure*, at the same time that it acts as a person *de facto*. This was the principle of the Taff Vale decision, which made Trade Unions responsible as such for their collective acts. On the other hand the same doctrine will enfranchise associations. We shall hold that associations which are living and acting like persons under social recognition are actually persons in virtue of such recognition; we shall not hold, like Lord Halsbury in the Osborne judgment, that Trade Unions can only exist through a charter of incorporation or within the limits of a statute. But our doctrine will not exempt such associations from the control of the State. The State, as a general and embracing scheme of life, must necessarily adjust the relations of associations to itself, to other associations, and to their own members—to itself, in order to maintain the integrity of its own scheme; to other associations, in order to preserve the equality of associations before the law; and to their own members, in order to preserve the individual from the possible tyranny of the group. Thus (1) the State will not even tolerate the existence of associations like the Mafia which are hostile to social life and public policy. Such associations, since they are not based on any common conviction or social recognition, are not persons, and their suppression is not the suppression of persons. In the same way, and on the same ground, the State will not tolerate such modes of action of recognised associations as fundamentally contradict its own purposes. (2) The State will proceed as far as possible on the principle of equality of associations; it will not readily tolerate the possession by one association of a privileged and exceptional position which other associations do not enjoy. (3) The State will demand from an association that it shall have a definite basis of action, and that such a basis shall be unitary, in the sense of not combining different kinds of action. If the State does not exact a definite basis, members of the association will not know to what they are pledged; if it does not demand a unitary basis, members who join the association for one kind of action of which they approve will have a just complaint, if they are forced to join in another kind of action of which they disapprove. If we apply these principles to Trade Unions, we may see what they involve. In the first place the State will have to decide whether the use of the funds of Trade Unions to support pledged members in Parliament is compatible with the public policy of England, or whether the purposes of parliamentary representation are contravened by the exaction of political pledges. In the second place, the State will have to decide whether the freedom from certain kinds of legal action, claimed by Trade Unions and conceded by the Trades Disputes Act of 1906, is compatible with the principle of equality of associations. Finally, the State will have to decide whether a Trade Union which combines political action, and a levy for political action, with economic action and an economic levy, is not combining different kinds of action, and failing to maintain a unitary basis; and whether, by such procedure, it may not be coercing unduly those of its members who approve of the one kind of action, and disapprove of the other.

These considerations may lead us to see that we must not push too far our claims on behalf of group-persons. Any unqualified theory of the " inherent rights " of associations is likely to do as much harm as the unqualified theory of the inherent or natural rights of the individual man once did. No rights are so inherent that they have not to be adjusted to other rights; and by the process of adjustment they become socially modified and socially controlled rights. We must beware of any plea for the inherent rights whether of Trade Unions or churches, unless such a plea is urged with due regard to the needs of adjustment. But with this proviso we may say that all the emphasis recently laid on rights of association suggests lines of thought which are valuable and likely to be fruitful.

Benthamite individualism treated the State too much as a compound of single units, and remembered too little the existence of its constituent groups. It was not over-tender to churches : and if its influence helped to emancipate Trade Unions, a Benthamite like Place could regard Trade Unions as temporary necessities, destined to make way for individual competition. We are beginning to lose this point of view. If we are individualists now, we are corporate individualists. Our " individuals " are becoming groups. No longer do we write *The Man versus the State :* we write *The Group versus the State.* There is much talk of federalism in these days. Behind the talk lies a feeling that the single unitary State, with its single sovereignty, is a dubious conception, which is hardly true to the facts of life. Every State, we feel, is something of a federal society, and contains within its borders different national groups, different churches, different economic organisations, each exercising its measure of control over its members. This federalistic feeling is curiously widespread. The newest Socialism has abandoned the paths of a unitary collectivism managed from a single centre. It cultivates the group under the name of the guild. While it recognises the State as the final owner of the means of production, it claims for each guild of workers in the same occupation the right to control as trustees the use of those means ; while it leaves to the State the promotion of culture, it claims for the guild the control of economic life. In this new Socialism the claim of Trade Unions to be free groups, freely developing their life in pursuit of

their own purposes—the claim urged during the
reaction against the Taff Vale judgment, and
largely recognised by parliamentary legislation
since 1906—finds its apogee. The same movement which appears in the new Socialism economically appears politically in the new Liberalism.
The core of that Liberalism would appear to be
a new federalism, not directed, as federalism
used to be, towards the integration of several
small States into a larger whole, but rather towards the disintegration of the great State into
smaller national groups on which large powers
are to be conferred by way of devolution.
Such at any rate is the lesson which the policy
of Liberalism in Ireland, in Wales, and to some
extent in Scotland, would seem to suggest.
Meanwhile a movement, possibly academic and
not of any great extent, seems to be setting towards the vindication of the rights of the religious group; and we may perhaps detect in
Dr. Figgis the ally in the religious sphere of the
policy which in the economic sphere appears as
Guild Socialism, and in the political sphere as
the new Liberalism.

It would be absurd to attribute these movements to any single influence. All this groping after guild socialism or syndicalism, federalism or Home Rule, rights of churches or disestablishment of churches, belongs to a general
trend of opinion which perhaps found its first
expression in France, and in the economic field,
but which has since spread to England and into
wider fields. With this trend of opinion the
legal theory from which we started—the theory
of the personality and the rights of the group—
is intimately connected; but the legal theory

is only one current in the general trend. We
seem to be living in days in which we are called
upon to revise in every direction our old conceptions of the State. We see the State in-
vited to retreat before the advance of the guild,
the national group, the Church. Yet whatever
rights such groups may claim or gain, the State
will still remain a necessary adjusting force;
and it is even possible that if groups are destined
to gain new ground, the State will also gain,
perhaps even more than it loses, because it will
be forced to deal with ever graver and ever
weightier problems of adjustment.

CHAPTER VII

THE POLITICAL THEORY OF LITERATURE

THE great voices in English literature
after 1848 were all raised against the
" anarchy " of laissez-faire. Matthew Arnold
was as anxious as Thomas Carlyle to replace
the rule of Manchester by the rule of wisdom;
and Dickens could denounce political economy
as fervently as Ruskin. The whole doctrine
of individualism was to the artist hard and
crude—unlovely in its insistence on axioms
as rigid as those of Euclid; repellent in its
mathematical calculus of utility; unsym-
pathetic in its attitude to human sentiments
and aspirations. Already in 1829 the poet
laureate, Southey, was preaching the tenets
of philanthropic collectivism, and his *Colloquies*
showed an antipathy to laissez-faire which was
to influence Lord Shaftesbury. The literary
tradition of Southey was continued in the

novels of Kingsley and Mrs. Gaskell, of Dickens and Charles Reade; and it appears, if in new forms, in the philippics of Carlyle and the delicate satire of Arnold.

Years before 1848 Carlyle was already far removed from Benthamism. In *Chartism* (1839) and in *Past and Present* (1843) his characteristic tenets are already to be found. " To button your pockets and stand still " is no true philosophy : what the working classes need is actual guidance and governance. Guidance being of all things necessary, Carlyle condemned democracy, which he identified with laissez-faire, as " a self-cancelling business," a government which only achieved the negation of any government. Representative institutions, a free and broad electorate, in a word all the paraphernalia of democracy, were in his eyes a matter of mere palaver and ballot-boxes—" nothing except emptiness " and zero. To get governance, men must turn to those who were able to govern, the silent few, standing aloof and alone in their wisdom, who were nature's appointed Hero-Kings. " There is in every community a fittest, a wisest, bravest, best; whom could we find and make king over us, all were in very truth well." Carlyle provides no method or machinery for his discovery : only a regeneration of our own hearts, which makes us heroic enough to recognise a Hero, can find for us our proper kings. Such kings, Carlyle believes, are essentially men of wisdom, with seeing eyes that discern the inner truth of things through all its vestures; but just for that reason they are also men of duty, guided by that moral sense, which only comes through depth of insight. Wise, and in their wisdom also virtuous, they must guide and even drill their lesser fellows, who shall find in obedience their chief end and highest pleasure.

Hating parliamentary reform, and hating the Whigs for riding that " dead horse " round and round, Carlyle passed over to the Tory camp. " Let the Tories be Ministry if they will : let at least some living reality be Ministry." He even travelled some way to Socialism. " The progress of human society consists even in this same, the better and better apportioning of wages to work." Guid-ance, regulation, drill became his ideals : military metaphors recur in his writings. He even advanced to the military doctrine that might is the measure of right. If a man be able, wise of heart, strong of will, firm in his resolution to do his duty among his fellows, he must govern according to the measure of his strength, and his right over his fellows is according to his might. " The strong thing is the just thing " : rights are " correctly articu-lated mights." Not that Carlyle worshipped force. On the contrary, he is so strongly convinced of the rule of justice in the spiritual world, that he cannot but think that all rule must in its nature be just. He is so sure that right is might, that he does not hesitate to say that might is right. God has so ordered and disposed the world in a just hierarchy, that all men who, by God's inner grace and endowment, and not by mere convention or electoral machinery, are called to be kings, stand justified in all their doings. The might of Frederick the Great or of Cromwell is God's

endowment. Because it is, it cannot but be
counted unto them for righteousness.

When he wrote his *Latter Day Pamphlets*
(1850) and *Shooting Niagara* (1867), Carlyle
still trod, with added vehemence and increased
extravagance, along old paths of thought.
Full of a burning thirst for reality and the
inner verity that lies behind semblance, he
storms impatiently through all the forms and
conventions in which democratic government
necessarily abounds, and rushes indignantly
to the abiding principle at the central heart
of things—let the fittest to rule bear rule. In
vain to urge that the seeming straightest path
does not always arrive; in vain to urge that
our complicated methods of election are, however roundabout, the best practical way we
have found of arriving at the fittest ruler.
Carlyle is determined to go straight. In his
haste to go straight, he only contrives to fall
into the ditch. In *Sartor Resartus* he had once
denounced the pheasant-shooting British aristocracy : in *Shooting Niagara* he seems willing
to find in the British aristocracy the " few
wise to take command of the innumerable
foolish." He praises their manners, the outward index of a kingly capacity within; and
with that love for the middle ages which he
had already shown in *Chartism* (as when he
wrote that " the old aristocracy were the
governors of the lower classes, the guides of
the lower classes ") and still more in *Past and
Present*, he sketches a new feudalism, somewhat
on the lines of Disraeli and the party of Young
England. The aristocracy might, each member in his own domain and land-territory,

become kings and fashioners of order. They might found schools, not of the " vocal " sort which teach men merely to talk and write, but of a practical kind that shall teach men how to behave and to do their work in life. They might drill their tenants, physically and morally, into the beauty of order and " combined rhythmic action "; they might even drill them in military exercises, and form a feudal levy ready to stand for order against radical anarchy. Not only through the landed aristocracy, drilling its tenants by technical education and military service, but also through the captains of industry, the " practical Heroes," might salvation come. " By intermarriage and otherwise " the industrial king will come into contact with the aristocracy by title; and meanwhile within his own sphere he may begin to work on the same lines of education and drill. For greater convenience of drill his men are to be tied to him by a permanent connection. " Nomadic contract " must pass into permanent : the mere weekly contract for wages must be changed into permanent servantship, if it can be managed. The whole society, so ordered and drilled, may have at its head three of the aristocracy and three of the industrial captains, with three of the heroes of speculation, or prophets of thought, as possible *amici curiæ*. Meanwhile, English colonies, at present lost in a fog of sham self-government, might be ordered and governed by English nobles or princes, ruling as colonial vice-kings and founding new houses with hereditary title.

A disciplined society, at one " in the silent

charm of rhythmic human companionship, in
the practical feeling . . . that all of us are
made on one pattern "; a society governed
from above by its ablest and best—this is
Carlyle's ideal. His abhorrence is that liberty
of which John Stuart Mill had written in the
Essay of 1859. " Divine commandment to
vote (' Manhood Suffrage '—Horsehood, Dog-
hood, ditto not yet treated of); universal
' glorious Liberty' (to Sons of the Devil in
overwhelming majority, it would appear); . . .
' the equality of men,' any man equal to any
other, Quashee Nigger to Socrates or Shake-
speare "—against all these beliefs he hurls his
scorn. For free trade (" free-racing," as
he prefers to say, " in the career of Cheap
and Nasty ") he has no less contempt. Of
what avail is the individualist policy of cutting
away from the horse the old traces, which are
so far from galling that they have become
comfortable, when there is no man with
enough of the hero or king to ride the horse?

In all this attitude, apart from its extrava·
gance of expression, there is a curious Platon-
ism. The love of ordered rhythm is Platonic.
The criticism of democracy, as a thing unstable
and nugatory, is again Platonic. The Hero
of Carlyle is the philosopher King of Plato.
Both opposed to democracy, Plato and Carlyle
are none. the less both radicals, anxious to
pluck up society by the roots and plant it
afresh in new soil : and if the new soil chosen
by Plato is more definitely socialistic, Carlyle,
in his attitude to competition and his desire
for permanence of contract, shows signs of a
socialistic trend. The likeness is not acci-

dental; it has its fundamental grounds.
Carlyle is of modern thinkers the most akin to
Plato, because he has the most vivid sense of
the spiritual reality of the universe.   As Plato
denounces in the *Gorgias* the shams and
simulacra which usurp the place of truth, so
Carlyle denounces in *Sartor Resartus* the
clothes and quackeries which hide the light;
and just as Plato denounces the oratory which
professes to be the essence of politics, so
Carlyle denounces the palavers and talking-
shops which pretend to be the way of government.   Both hasten from the phenomenal
world to the divine Idea which alone is true;
both hope for the realisation of that Idea in
the realm of politics by the hero who has seen
and has attained unto wisdom.   Plato, it is
true, would equip his hero by a rigorous course
of study, and would trust to that study for
the discovery of the true " aristocracy of
talent "; Carlyle, less of a dialectician and
more of an intuitionalist, seems to dream of a
hero armed at birth with a divine intuition,
and discovered by hazard or the intuition of
society.   Here Plato and Carlyle diverge; but
they reunite in a magnificent impatience, which
would fain capture the ideal by a frontal
assault at all hazards and in one sweep. ˙ Not
content with an Idea somehow immanent in
society, and transforming it slowly after its
own likeness, they would have the Idea
elicited and the society shaped consciously to
its norm; not content with the slow democratic
process by which society seeks to discover by
its own choice its own best for its governance,
they would enthrone the best by a sort of

coup d'état. Neither will trust in a tardy grinding of the mills; neither has confidence in the slow but sure workings of a collective intelligence. Both take their stand as opponents of democracy : both tend to forget that only the society that achieves its own salvation is saved. Neither, it is true, condemns the fundamental end of democracy, that every man should have his fulfilment in the State; that, on the contrary, is their own fundamental aim. But both neglect the only means by which that aim can ever be secured; for both fail to recognise that every man must have a voice in his own fulfilment. No believer in democracy would deny the great contention of Plato and Carlyle, that the aristocracy of the ablest and best should rule; but most believers in democracy would doubt whether such an aristocracy can be found by any other means than the free choice of all.

Ruskin combined the artist's longing for beauty with the moralist's passion for social justice. Like Morris, he came to the study of social problems by the way of art. Morris felt that social life must be remoulded to make beauty at once deeper and more widely diffused; Ruskin felt that art, which is ultimately the expression of national character, needed for its perfection the cleansing of national character, and, to that end, a remodelling of all the institutions of social life which go to determine national character. Morris preached that good workmanship was only possible to free and joyous workers, and that free and joyous workers were only possible in a socialistic state : Ruskin taught that art

can only be good and beautiful, when it grows
out of a world of social and political life which
is also good and beautiful. " Art not for
art's sake, but art in relation to life; art as
the expression of individual and of national
character; life without industry as guilt, but
industry without art as brutality; beauty in
a world governed by social justice; these are
ideas implied in all Ruskin's books." But
Ruskin was not only an artist; he was also
a thinker who sat at the feet of " the Master,"
Thomas Carlyle, and who had drunk deep
of that Platonic philosophy to which, as we
have seen, the Master's teaching was itself so
closely akin. Like Carlyle, Ruskin preached
the supremacy of the spirit in an age of materialism; like Carlyle, he preached the supreme
need of finding and trusting wise governors,
though, again like Carlyle, he supplied few clues
for their discovery. Above all, he was led by
his study of Plato and other Greek thinkers
to become the apostle of what may be termed
a Greek theory of economics. To the Greeks,
as one may read in the writings of Plato and
Xenophon and Aristotle, economics is no
separate and independent study; on the contrary, it is a subordinate branch of that great
art of politics, which is concerned with the
moral betterment of political society. Economics, they hold, cannot be considered by itself;
it must be considered in connection with
ethics, for it deals with wealth not as an end
in itself to be used by the individual just as
he will, but as a " collection of tools " to be
used by each member of society as means for
the living of a good and beautiful social life.

This is exactly the view of economics which
Ruskin set himself to champion in the nineteenth century. He too would fain subordinate
wealth to life—the more eagerly and the more
drastically, because he felt that no beauty of
life was possible when wealth became the
master, and ceased to be the servant, of life.

As early as 1857 Ruskin was daring enough
to deliver in Manchester itself, the home of
economic orthodoxy, a series of lectures in
which he attacked the cult of wealth and
the worship of competition. These lectures,
printed originally under the title of *The
Political Economy of Art*, but reprinted afterwards under the new title of *A Joy for Ever*,
already contain some of Ruskin's cardinal
tenets. They advocate co-operation ("as in
a household "—the very analogy used by
Plato) in lieu of competition; they advocate
State-education, State-employment, and State-
provision for the old age of the labourer.
" Government and co-operation are the laws
of life; anarchy and competition the laws of
death." To fulfil the law of life, the workers
must become like unto soldiers. They must
be trained like soldiers, and like soldiers they
must be guided. In those days men shall
speak of " soldiers of the Ploughshare as well
as soldiers of the Sword." Teaching of this
order shocked an age given over to the doctrine
of laissez-faire; and critics applied to Ruskin
the strictures which Macaulay had passed on
Southey. He would make the State, they
said, " a jack-of-all-trades . . . a Lady Bounti-
ful in every parish, a Paul Pry in every house."
Undeterred by his critics, Ruskin in 1860

published a new essay " on the first principle of political economy " under the title of *Unto this Last.* In this—perhaps his best and certainly his most classical book on social matters —Ruskin seeks to banish to limbo the abstract " economic man " of the economist, and to establish the principle that the only man whom science can consider is the whole man— man with all his social affections, man in all his social relations. He seeks to moralise political economy, and to give it its due place as a subordinate science faithfully serving the sovereign science of politics in its high and final function of creating good citizenship. With this end in view he appeals once more to the State to assume a wider province of action; to educate its citizens in the laws of health, in manners and morals, and in good craftsmanship; to start Government workshops for " authoritatively good and exemplary work "; to put the unemployed compulsorily to work; to provide comfort and homes for the old and destitute. Laissez-faire must disappear at the window, and a wise paternalism enter at the door. The wise merchant must recognise that he " is invested with a distinctly paternal authority and responsibility " for the lives of his men : the wise thinker must strive to preach " the eternal superiority of some men to others, sometimes even of one man to all others; and to show also the advisability of appointing such persons or person to guide, to lead, or on occasion even to compel and subdue, their inferiors according to their own better knowledge and wiser will."

Unto this Last, even if it be not, as Mr.

G

Frederic Harrison has said, " the most original and creative work in pure literature since *Sartor Resartus*," at any rate marks, as Ruskin himself believed, the height of his achievement. In other and later works he added little but detail to his doctrine. In *Munera Pulveris* (1863) he attacked the conceptions of wealth which were held by orthodox economists. In *Time and Tide*, which was published in 1867, the year of the Second Reform Bill, he vindicated the priority of social regeneration to political reform, and urged, in the spirit of Carlyle, that the condition of England was a matter of more vital concern than constituencies and ballot-boxes. In *Fors Clavigera*, a series of monthly letters to working men, written between 1871 and 1878 under the influence of Carlyle, and with something of the fury which his Master had shown in *Past and Present*, Ruskin criticised the condition of his age, and " endeavoured to show the conditions under which alone great art (itself the product of the happy life of the workman) was possible " in the future.   During the same period was founded St. George's Guild—with Ruskin for its Master ; with eight vows for its members, embracing the articles of Ruskin's creed ; and with a practical policy (which in the issue came to very little) of acquiring land for settlement by labourers who should enjoy fixed rents and decent conditions of life.   It is curious to notice how these projected settlements, which were to be under the control of a landed aristocracy enforcing " the beneficency of strict military order," correspond to the teaching of Carlyle in *Shooting Niagara.*

Ruskin was no more a Socialist than Carlyle. He did not believe in that democratic control of economic life, which is the vital article of Socialist faith : he did not believe in the nationalisation of land, but rather in inducing landlords so to use their land, as to produce the true wealth which consists in good and beautiful human lives. Nevertheless in many ways he prepared the ground for Socialism. By the charm of his style and the vogue of his writings he spread far and wide, among all classes, a feeling of distrust in the old individualistic political economy. He taught thousands of readers to criticise the abstraction of the economic motive on which it rested, and to believe in the necessity of starting from the whole man, compact of social affection as well as of economic motive, in any pursuit of economic study. Again he turned men's thought and attention from the accumulation to the use of wealth. He taught that it is not the getting, but the spending of wealth that matters; that the end of the State is not the clearing of the way in order that the economic man may have free scope in production, but an adjustment of conditions such that the whole man may have room for the use of his tools for the building of the life beautiful. Such teaching has influenced the doctrines of pure economics. It has helped to turn economists since the days of Jevons from the theory of production to the theory of consumption; it has helped to correct the old emphasis laid on saving, and to give more weight to spending; it has helped to modify the old conception of value as mainly deter-

mined by cost of production, and to give more
scope to the influence of utility in the creation
of value. Nor has Ruskin's teaching only
influenced economic science; it has also
affected the theory and the practice of politics.
When Ruskin began to write, laissez-faire
was as much a political dogma, as it was an
economic doctrine. His writings undermined
the doctrine in both of its applications. He
pleaded for an extension of State-interference,
alike in the education of the young, the
employment of the adult, and the relief of
the aged; and the vogue of his writings
enabled him, perhaps more than any other
writer, to help men to shed the old distrust of
the State, and to welcome, as men since 1870
have more and more welcomed, the activity of
society on behalf of its members. If Ruskin was
not the begetter of English Socialism, he was a
foster-father to many English Socialists.

Nevertheless, he remains a Platonist rather
than a Socialist. He was more interested in
the *Economist* of Xenophon than the *Capital*
of Marx. Like his Greek teachers, but with
less excuse than they, he fell into the error
of denouncing the whole process of exchange
as nugatory. His political teaching, in its
strength and in its weakness, is essentially
Platonic. He had all Plato's ardour for
education, and much of Plato's own theory
of education. He urged, and he helped to
convince England, that the aim and object
of education is behaviour, and not knowledge;
character, rather than mere intelligence; in a
word, " the perfect exercise and kingly conti-
nence of body and soul." Like Plato, he

sought to assign a large scope to æsthetic influence. The need for the study of beautiful nature; the need for surrounding the child in the school-room with beautiful pictures and works of art; the need for training in music and dancing, " the two primal instruments of education," are all recurrent themes. He is more modern, though he is not therefore any the less Platonic, when he pleads for practical and technical training in arts and crafts, and when again he demands teaching in what we should nowadays call civics—" the science of the relations and duties of men to each other " —which, he thought, might best be studied in Xenophon's *Economist*. But zeal for the perfect circle of a rounded education does not with Ruskin, any more than with Plato, ally itself with any belief in democracy. He cannot hold, like Mill, that in and through the use of the franchise the citizen receives an incomparable education of thought and of will. The rule of the wisest is his ideal; and the populace is apparently neither wise itself nor able to select the wise. How the wise should be found, Ruskin, like his master Carlyle, did not and could not disclose. " Hasting stormfully " towards that consummation, " in which the Sun of Justice shines upon gracious laws of beauty and labour," he left the means to its attainment either unexplained, or outlined in fanciful adumbrations like the sketch for the organisation of St. George's Guild, with its Master and Marshals, its Landlords and Companions. Ways and means are not for the prophets. But it is the worst of prophets like Carlyle and Ruskin that, despising the ways and means of democracy, they fall back into something of an obscurantist alliance with reaction. It did not greatly help the Glasgow undergraduates to be told by Ruskin, when they suggested to him an election address, " you have no more business with politics than you have with rat-catching . . . but I hate all Liberalism as I do Beelzebub, and with Carlyle I stand, we two now alone in England, for God and the Queen."

The influence of Carlyle was on the whole in favour of authoritarianism; and the teaching of Matthew Arnold ran the same way. But while Carlyle sought the aid of authority to realise divine justice, Arnold enlisted authority to defend the sweetness and light of culture against the tasteless riot of an individualistic age. In *Culture and Anarchy* (1869) it is the artist rather than the moralist who is in revolt against " Manchesterdom "; and Arnold is in this sense the fellow of Ruskin and Morris. But he lays his finger more definitely than his successors on a central fact of English politics—the English inability, partly due to long centuries of Dissent, partly due to the economics of laissez-faire, to form any idea of the State, " the nation in its collective and corporate capacity controlling as government the full swing of its members in the name of the higher reason of all." In order to enthrone right reason, Arnold argues for the rule neither of the aristocracy of barbarians, nor of the middle class of philistines, nor of the populace, but of an authority which represents our best selves made perfect by culture. Where such an authority may be

found he will not decide; he lays his main
emphasis on the duty of attaining self-perfec-
tion through culture in order to make such an
authority possible. But when he argues for
an authoritative centre, like an Academy, in
the field of literature; when he urges that
representative government issues in pandering
to the populace instead of the rule of right
reason; when he praises the work done by
an absolute monarchy in Prussia for the cause
of education, his inclination seems clear. In
the name of good taste or right reason he seeks
an authority which will not pander to the
bad taste of any class, and which must therefore
presumably, be non-representative; and it is
difficult to see where such an authority can be
found except in a sort of absolute monarchy.
Arnold would have instantly denied that he
sought anything of this order; he would have
treated the idea with elusive and delicate irony;
and yet this is the one logical issue of his teaching.

The authoritarianism which appears in Carlyle and Ruskin and Arnold also marks the
English Positivists, who have followed the
teaching of Comte. Positivism in England
dates from 1848, when Congreve, a Fellow of
Wadham College, Oxford, visited Paris and
came under the influence of Comte. Three other
members of the same college, Mr. Beesly, Dr.
Bridges, and Mr. Frederic Harrison, became
followers of Congreve's example and Comte's
teaching. English Positivism, however, has
remained something of an esoteric creed; and
it has been rather directed to the profession
of faith in the Religion of Humanity than to
the enunciation of a political creed. So far

as its followers have preached politics, they have simply expounded the tenets of their master. Differing from Plato in his rejection of all metaphysical principles, and refusing to accept any but positive principles drawn by induction from the past and the present, Comte was nevertheless a Platonist in his belief in the reconstruction of the State, and in the guidance of that reconstructed State, by the light of scientific principles. Somewhat like Plato, again, though influenced by the mediæval church more than by Plato, he drew a distinction between the spiritual and the temporal power, the spiritual and temporal class. His ideal State would have been one in which the spiritual class, " a combination of *savans* orthodox in science," expressive of reason and acting by persuasion rather than force, guided the course of affairs in the light of scientific principles.

In his youth Comte had been in close association with St. Simon, and it was from St. Simon that he drew his conviction that the goal of philosophy must be social, and its work the regeneration of society; while it was also to St. Simon that he was largely indebted for his distinction between the spiritual and the temporal power. St. Simon is counted among the founders of Socialism and the advocates of the party of labour; and though Comte himself hardly followed St. Simon in these channels, one of his own theses was the passing away of the old military régime to make room for a new régime of industry. It is thus not surprising to find one of Comte's English disciples, Prof. Beesly, presiding in 1864 at the meeting which heard Marx's "Inaugural" and saw the foundation of the International, or joining with Hyndman in the beginnings of a British Socialist party immediately after 1880. Congreve, who in some ways departed from the other English Positivists, followed a different line. In one of the essays appended to his edition of Aristotle's *Politics* (1855) he advocates, as a temporary measure, to prepare the way for the ultimate ideal, government by a dictator resting on a plébiscite. Such a dictator, he argues, representing the growing proletariate while defending the decadent aristocracy, will mediate between both; fostering discussion and encouraging progress, he will bridge the transition to the new organisation which industrialism will require and evolve. It is this sense for authority, this feeling for the necessity of wise direction from above, which is one of the fundamental tenets of English Positivism, as it is one of the fundamental tenets of Comte.

No other men of letters have exercised the influence in English politics which was exercised by Carlyle and Ruskin. But the literary tradition throughout the period under survey has on the whole followed the same lines which we have attempted to trace in their writings. Literature, when it has turned to social and political life, has been a criticism of the condition of England, and a suggestion for social reconstruction by an authoritative state. Dickens, in earlier days a representative of Radical thought, was already in 1854 delivering in *Hard Times* an attack on individualist economics which drew a warm encomium from Ruskin. Froude continued the tradition of Carlyle, and found in strong men the saviours of society. Publicists, from W. R. Greg in his *Essays on Political and Social Science* (1853) to W. E. H. Lecky in his *Democracy and Liberty* (1898), stood for order rather than progress, aristocracy rather than democracy. What Lord Morley says of Greg, whom he accounts " one of the literary representatives of the fastidious or pedantocratic school of government," may stand for many others: " His ideal, like that of most literary thinkers on politics, was an aristocracy not of caste, but of education, virtue and public spirit . . . the old dream of lofty minds from Plato down to Turgot." Whether Lord Morley himself, a shining and venerable name, should be called a literary thinker on politics, or a politician who is also a great literary thinker, we need not discuss. It is clear at any rate that the author of *Compromise*, like Lord Bryce, has been able to combine the power of literary thought with a firm faith in democracy.

The literary prophets of our own days may perhaps seem rebels rather than servants of authority. Belloc, Shaw and Wells are hardly defenders of social order. To discuss the tenets which by pamphlet or essay, drama or novel, they inculcate or imply belongs more properly to the next chapter. Here it may not be amiss to say one thing. Shaw and Wells have both been conspicuous figures in the history of Socialism. Carlyle and Ruskin were not Socialists, but they did more to spread thoughts that prepared the way for Socialism than any other English writers. A Socialist like Mr. Will Thorne can quote Carlyle in his election

address in 1906; the Labour members of the
Parliament of 1906, many of whom were
Socialists, confessed that they had found the
chief literary influence of their lives in one of
Ruskin's books. It seems quite consonant
with historical continuity that some of the
foremost literary men of our days should be
definite Socialists. Those who aim at the
lucidus ordo of thought in their own writings
are impelled by an inner logic to seek in social
life the beauty of order and the charm of
definition. Ruskin and Carlyle sought that
beauty and charm in one way; our modern
men of letters tend to seek it along another
line. But whatever the difference, the man
of letters remains by nature a Platonist in
politics. Even Mr. Belloc, ardent anarchist as
he seems in his attack on the servile State,
and curious as is his mixture of catholicism,
syndicalism and a belief in peasant proprietor-
ship, is at bottom true to the literary tradition.
He would substitute for mere capitalist
anarchy, not, indeed, the servile State beloved
by some of his fellow-craftsmen, but at any
rate a *system*—a system of well-divided property, of ordered co-operative guilds, and, behind all and above all, the old Faith, once
more reinstated in its intimate and guiding
place in the heart of Europe.

CHAPTER VIII

ECONOMICS AND POLITICS

INDIVIDUALISM, resting primarily on Bentham, but buttressed by the economics of

laissez-faire, continued to be the political creed of most English writers and thinkers till about 1880. Other tendencies had, indeed, already appeared before that date. Legislation, according to Prof. Dicey, had become perceptibly " collectivist " about 1870, when Mr. Forster passed the first Education Act. The public opinion which lies behind legislation had been moving towards socialistic ideas at a still earlier date. It is true that, after Chartism died in 1848, there was no longer any large movement of the working classes for the reorganisation of society. There were many strikes in the 'sixties, and in the 'seventies the Trade Unions claimed and gained from Parliament a new freedom by the Acts of 1871 and 1876; but on the whole the working classes abandoned any separate interest in politics, and passed into the left wing of the Liberal Army. Nevertheless, there was a constant protest from many quarters against the gospel of individualism and laissez-faire between 1848 and 1880. Carlyle did not cease to denounce that gospel, or to plead for " an aristocracy of talent," wisely directing society, and for " the better and better apportioning of wages to work." Again, there were the Christian Socialists, who, it has been said, tolled the bell at the funeral of Chartism. The year 1850 saw the publication of the *Tracts on Christian Socialism* and of Kingsley's *Alton Locke ;* but the Christian Socialism of Maurice and Kingsley had only a brief life of some four years. More serious was the activity of Marx, who in 1864, with the aid of Prof. Beesly, a Positivist, founded the International Society, and who in his inaugural address defined its aims as consisting in the independent action of the working classes and the international union of those classes for a socialistic reconstruction of society. The " International," however, had little influence on England in the course of its troubled existence; and the influence of Marx himself was not seriously felt until after 1880.

It is rather in the inner development of individualism itself, than through the action of any external forces, that opinion has been revolutionised. Bentham had advocated two principles not altogether consistent with one another. On the one hand, he had advocated the principle, which belongs chiefly to the economic field, of the right of each man to pursue his own interest; on the other hand, he had urged, in the political sphere, the right and duty of the State to secure the greatest happiness of the greatest number. Time was destined to emphasise the second of these principles at the expense of the first. Not only was the principle of laissez-faire denounced by Carlyle; it was actually repudiated by the State, under the guidance of men like Lord Shaftesbury, in a series of Factory Acts. The change became still more striking, when Southey, " the prophetic precursor of modern collectivism," was succeeded by John Stuart Mill himself in that rôle. As early as 1848, in his *Principles of Political Economy*, Mill recognised that distribution was a matter of artificial arrangement which might be regulated by the State, and advocated taxation of the unearned increment of land. Here he laid the foundations on which the Fabian party was

destined to build. The *Essay on Liberty* (1859)
was, it is true, a fine vindication of spiritual
liberty and originality against restraints
whether of legislation or of social opinion; but
the trend towards something like State Socialism still remained; and in his Autobiography
Mill tells us that he looked forward to a time
when " the division of the produce of labour . . .
will be made by concert on an acknowledged
principle of justice." In his Essay on *Utilitarianism* (1863) he so far abandoned the principle
of self-interest as to adopt the principle of self-
sacrifice. " To serve the happiness of others
by the absolute sacrifice of his own," was, he
felt, in the present very imperfect state of the
world's arrangements, " the highest virtue that
can be found in man."

A transitional thinker, full of the incon-
sistencies natural to a period of transition, but
supremely candid and generous in all his
inconsistency, Mill prepared above all others
the way for the new development of English
thought which appears after 1880. A book
which also served to aid that development
was Prof. Jevons' *The State in Relation to
Labour*, which was published in 1882. Jevons
throws overboard any fixed principles whether
of natural rights or of laissez-faire. You cannot
solve any particular issue on which the intervention of the State is demanded or denounced
in the light of such general principles. You
can only proceed empirically, and take each
case on its merits. " Every single Act ought
to be judged separately as regards the balance
of good or evil which it produces." Such an
empirical judgment must necessarily assume a

quantitative form; it must enumerate the facts which have to be balanced on either side, and then proceed to make its computation accordingly. The statesman must leave legislation based on first principles for Baconian legislation resting on the ground of experience; and to understand that experience he must measure the factors which it reveals by a mathematical process. Jevons thus pointed the way to that method of " legislation by statistics " which has become the general rule during the last thirty years. He introduced no new dogma; he simply assumed the old Benthamite principle that the general welfare of the community is the canon of all legislation. He did not really introduce a new method : he went back to a method as old as Bacon. But his influence has been considerable. Statesmen of 1834 faced the problem of the poor law with the aid of the first principles of individualism. Statesmen eighty years later face the same problem with the aid of hundreds of pages of statistics. But if he introduced no new dogma to supersede the old dogma of laissez-faire, Jevons emancipated himself from the old economic belief that the balance was always against the interference of the State; and he taught, and helped others to believe, that there was no presupposition either for or against State-interference. The liberty of the individual was not an end in itself, but a means to the general welfare; and if, on a calculation of the factors which enable men to forecast the results of a given policy on the general welfare, the balance was against individual liberty, that liberty must make room for the intervention of the State.

After 1880 the bankruptcy of the old Benthamite Liberalism was beginning to be apparent. New ideals were needed for the new classes which had won the franchise. If the parliamentary middle class which had been emancipated in 1832 had been content with Benthamism, the artisans admitted in 1867, and the labourers admitted in 1885, needed other fare. It is, indeed, curious to notice how the Third Reform Bill of 1884, and the constitutional difficulties between the two Houses which it provoked, served to precipitate opinion. On the one hand, as we have already seen, Spencer was alarmed into a vigorous defence of laissez-faire and " the man *versus* the state," and Maine was driven into a pessimistic criticism of popular government and an insistence upon the needs of checks and safeguards. On the other hand, a bolder school of thinkers felt encouragement rather than alarm; and Socialism, as a central force in English thought, and no longer as an eccentric opinion, now appears in the field. Economic factors may have aided its appearance : a wave of prosperity had spent itself about 1875, and in the stagnation which ensued new economic doctrines found a congenial environment.

Socialism, as it was first advocated, was a somewhat mechanical creed, which aimed at the sudden construction of Utopia on the ruins of the past. But Socialism of this type had already vanished in 1880. Under the influence of Karl Marx, a new evolutionary socialism, expecting no new heaven or new earth to be attained immediately—whether by workshops or by co-operation or by any other

means—had taken its place. Behind the
economic teaching of Marx lay a large view
of society. He regarded society not as artificial, but as living structure subject to growth
and decay. Human insight might detect,
and human effort might aid, the tendencies
of growth : what they could not do was
to take society to pieces and to put it together again. In this way Marx was led to
feel that the path of progress was not to be
found in a catastrophic change, but in reforms
which would aid the natural growth of society
towards a gradual social transformation—reforms each of which successively altered the
nature of the body social till their sum total
ultimately altered its quality altogether and
completed the revolution. Thus Socialism
under the influence of Marx came into alliance
with biology; and the alliance is most conspicuous to-day in the writings of Mr. Ramsay
Macdonald, who may be regarded as the
apostle of a definitely biological Socialism.

At the same time Marx did not by any means
hold a thoroughly organic view of the nature of
society. Society might to-day be growing by
an organic process : the ultimate society of the
future might be a pure organic unity; but as
things stood, with capital exploiting labour and
the workers deprived of their just reward, there
was a great gulf in every society between
masters and men, and the " class-consciousness " of the men could not but be utterly and
entirely opposed to that of the masters. Whatever Socialism triumphant might be, Socialism
militant meant a truceless war; and every
society was divided into two armies engaged in

that war, with the object on the one side of has-
tening, and on the other of defeating, the revolution which should inaugurate the final day.   On
the methods of this war differences of opinion
arose in the ranks of Socialists.   Some were
for international action, and Marx himself, as
we have seen, founded the International; some
were for separate national action.   Some intended a peaceful revolution achieved within
the ambit of the law : others spoke of dynamite
as destined to end capitalism in the same way
as gunpowder had ended feudalism.   Above
all, while some believed in political action—
that is to say, in the conquest of political power
by the masses, and the use of political power to
achieve the revolution piece-meal—others believed in purely economic action, advocating
strikes and the ultimate expropriation of capital,
and disdaining or eschewing the paths of politics.[1]   This divergence has indeed been constant
and fundamental in the ranks of Socialists; and
it was a defect of Marx himself that he was vague
in his political teaching, prone to emphasise the
negative concept of the class-war, but not so
ready to provide any constructive political
programme, and somewhat " negligent of the
necessities of government."   A certain in-
stability and vacillation has thus characterised
the organisations, such as the Social Democratic

---

[1] In European Socialism at large there is still a
cleavage between the Revolutionary and the Reformist
parties.   The one believes in the accomplishment of all
the aims of Socialism simultaneously as a system : the
other in the realisation of those aims successively and
piecemeal.   The one thinks in terms of the class-war :
the other in terms of the solidarity of classes.   *Cf.*
Ensor, *Modern Socialism*, pp. xxxiii *sqq.*

Federation and its successor the British Socialist Party, which have lived on the Marxian tradition. They can, indeed, discern firmly their goal : it is " the socialisation of the means of production, distribution, and exchange, the whole to be controlled by a democratically organised state in the interest of the entire community." About the means to its attainment they have always been dubious. They have sometimes advocated a policy of gradual reform and amelioration : they have sometimes denounced the policy of " palliatives " and " meliorism," because it lulled class-consciousness to sleep and postponed or killed the revolution. They have been willing and unwilling to co-operate with other bodies to gain political representation : they have been anxious and apathetic about separate political representation of their own views. They have feared Trade Unions as the props and pillars of meliorism ; and on the other hand, as recently as 1912, the British Socialist Party, caught by the new syndicalist fashion, was set on achieving a perfect industrial organisation through Trade Unions, and was advocating a policy of strengthening the unions in every way so that they should ultimately be capable of taking over the control of production in the Socialist state.

The definitely Marxian influence in England has been seen in the writings of Hyndman and in the propaganda of the Social Democratic Federation, of which the most striking figure was for many years William Morris. The beginnings of this phase date from 1881, when Hyndman published *England for All*, and founded the Social Democratic Federation. The Feder-

ation had a programme which included land
nationalisation, but which was also largely
concerned with political objects such as universal suffrage, payment of members, Home
Rule for Ireland and free parliaments for all
colonies and dependencies. Morris was an
early member, and he helped to edit a paper
called *Justice*, which was the organ of the
Federation. One of Morris's main motives
was his desire for the coming of a state of
society, in which loving workmanship and
creative art might thrive; and his passion for
Socialism was based largely on his belief, that
capitalism was the ruin of craftsmanship. He
was opposed to parliamentary action : Parliament, he felt, was always occupied in repairing
the social structure which it was the object
of Socialists to destroy. He was even opposed
to Trade Unions, because they served as buffers
between the Liberalism he detested and the
social revolution he desired. Differences of
opinion with Hyndman drove him and others
from the League (1884); and he joined in the
foundation of a new organisation, the Socialist
League, and in editing its organ, *The Commonwealth*. In 1890, however, the League was
captured by Anarchists, and Morris resigned his
membership; but before he left the League, he
wrote the finest of his socialistic writings—
News from Nowhere. Here, in the form of a
romance, he sketches the State of the future,
describing the violent revolution by which it
was created, and painting the joy and beauty
of the new life which it brought.[1]

[1] It is impossible, within the limits of this volume, to
give any account of the socialistic Utopias of Morris

Morris was something of a revolutionary Utopian. A brand-new society was, he imagined, to be built by a sudden effort; and meanwhile amelioration, whether pursued by parliamentary action or through Trade Unions, was to be avoided. Something of the same tendency has continued to dwell in the British Socialist Party, though it has wavered in its attitude—sometimes adopting, and sometimes denouncing, " palliatives "; now courting, now avoiding Trade Unions; at one time attempting, and at another time shunning, participation in politics. A different attitude appears when we turn to the Fabians, who founded their Society in 1884, and issued their *Essays* in 1889. The Fabians, of whom Sidney Webb and Bernard Shaw were the foremost members, had been influenced by Marx; but, as we shall see, it was by the evolutionary element of his teaching, rather than by the revolutionary idea which attracted Morris, that they were guided. On the whole, however, Mill rather than Marx was their starting-point. They do not begin, like Marx, by attacking capital as the stolen fruits of labour which have been filched by the capitalist from the working man : they start along the line suggested by Mill, with an attack on rent as the " unearned increment " of land,

---

and Wells, Bellamy and Blatchford. They belong to the sphere of economic prophecy rather than to political thought. All political theory is concerned with the State as it should be, and in that sense is concerned with ideals; but the explanation, in novelistic form, of the structural details of a Utopia is rather an essay of the imagination than an analysis of the ideals which underlie the action of the State.

which has been stolen (or at any rate abstracted)
by the landlord from the society which is its
creator, and to which it properly belongs.

In a word, it is land rather than capital which
has been the objective of English Socialism in
its peculiar and indigenous form; and this fact
suggests some reflections. The English system
of land-holding is peculiar; it is marked by the
aggregation in a few hands of large estates
as well urban as rural. This is an essential
feature of English economy which differentiates
English life greatly from that of the Continent,
where land is much more widely distributed.
Our social reformers have thus concentrated
their attack on landlords, who, it is urged, have
taken a large toll from the vast growth of
English wealth in the last hundred and fifty
years. We have already seen that T. H. Green,
while comparatively tender to capital, was adverse to the English system of landed property,
which he held responsible for the creation of a
" propertyless proletariate." The teaching of
Green had its precursors, and has had its successors. As early as 1775 Spence had preached
land nationalisation to the Philosophical Society
of Newcastle; and the Spenceans had continued
his tradition. In 1850 Dove, in a work on the
Science of Politics, had advocated the same
policy; and at the same time Herbert Spencer,
in his *Social Statics*, had argued against private
property in land. Mill, more particularly in
the later editions of his *Political Economy*, had
advanced from the Ricardian doctrine of rent,
as the sum paid to the landlord for the use of
the original and indestructible powers of the
soil, to his own theory of " unearned incre-

ment," a theory which readily passes into the doctrine of " socially created values "; while from socially created values it is an easy step to Socialism of the Fabian type. The American, Henry George, though adding no new ideas, had added new vigour and " hustle " to an old doctrine in his *Progress and Poverty* (1879); and Russel Wallace had also espoused the cause of land nationalisation.

This was the line of thought continued in Fabianism, though its founders drew inspiration from Proudhon in France and Marx in Germany as well as from their own soil.   But Mill's was the chief influence.   It is Mill who supplies the economic doctrine : it is Mill who serves, in the years between 1848 and 1880, as the bridge from laissez-faire to the idea of social readjustment by the State, and from political Radicalism to economic Socialism.   Drawing its inspiration from these sources, Fabianism began after 1884 to supply a new philosophy in place of Benthamite Individualism.   Of the new gospel of collectivism, a German writer has said, Webb was the Bentham and Shaw the Mill.   Without assigning rôles, we may fairly say there is some resemblance between the influence of Benthamism on legislation after 1830, and the influence of Fabianism on legislation since, at any rate, 1906.   In either case we have a small circle of thinkers and investigators, in quiet touch with politicians : in either case we have a " permeation " of general opinion by the ideas of these thinkers and investigators. As Bentham threw aside the old conception of natural rights for that of utility, so, if less drastically, the Fabians threw aside the older theory of value as based entirely on labour, and the older policy of the class-war, for a theory of marginal values based on utility, and a policy of the gradual socialisation of rent. As Bentham made his principle the greatest happiness of the greatest number, so the Fabians made their principle the social control of socially created values. Differences of course there are. Benthamism was prior to Benthamite legislation : legislation of a collectivist character preceded Fabianism by nearly twenty years. Benthamism came to be a generally accepted creed : Fabianism is only adopted openly by a small minority. None the less it is probable that the historian of the future will emphasise Fabianism in much the same way as the historian of to-day emphasises Benthamism.

Bentham was primarily concerned with legal and constitutional reform : Fabianism is primarily concerned with social and economic reform. But Fabianism has its own political creed, if it is a political creed consequential upon an economic doctrine. That economic doctrine advocates the socialisation of rent. But the rents which Fabians would socialise are not only rents from land. Rent, in the sense of unearned increment, may be drawn, and is drawn, from other sources. The successful entrepreneur, for instance, draws a rent of ability from his superior equipment and education. The socialisation of every kind of rent will necessarily arm the State with great funds which it must use. What kind of state will best be able to use these funds ? Not the old state which, whatever its form, was in fact an oligarchy, using the powers of the State to advance the interests of a class—a state from which men sought refuge in preaching laissez-faire and in limiting as far as in them lay the powers of its interference. *That* state is at once too selfish and too incompetent to be given fresh power; and collectivism demands a state which is neither selfish nor incompetent. Collectivism demands in the first place a purely democratic state. The wealth which has been created by the whole society must be owned and administered by the whole society. The private owner of rent, whether it was drawn from land or from industry, was able to dictate the conditions of life to his " hands "; the State as owner will equally be able to dictate conditions. Only if the State which dictates conditions to workers is itself the workers will freedom be attained. Then, and then only, will those who own the means of production be also the users of those means; then, and then only, will the people dictate to itself the conditions of such use. Thus will be realised, in a new sense, the ideal of Rousseau, that the governing people (the *Souverain*) should be one and the same as the governed people (the *État*), and that " each, giving the direction of himself to all, should give himself to none." And thus Shaw can define the two interconnected aims of Fabianism as " the gradual extension of the franchise and the transfer of rent and interest to the State."

But collectivism also demands, in the second place, expert government. It demands the " aristocracy of talent " of which Carlyle wrote. The control of a state with powers so vast will obviously need an exceptional and exceptionally

large aristocracy. Those opponents of Fabianism who desire something more revolutionary
than its policy of " meliorism " and " palliatives " accuse it of alliance with bureaucracy.
They urge that it relies on bureaucracy to
administer social reforms from above; and
they conclude that, since any governing *class* is
anti-democratic, the Fabians, who believe in
such a class, are really anti-democratic. The
charge seems, as a matter of fact, difficult to
sustain. Fabians from the first felt and urged
that the decentralisation of the State was a
necessary condition of the realisation of their
aim. The municipality and other local units
were the natural bodies for administering the
new funds and discharging the new duties
which the realisation of that aim would create.
" A democratic State," Shaw wrote, " cannot
become a Social-democratic State, unless it has
in every centre of population a local governing
body as thoroughly democratic in its constitution as the central parliament." The House of
Commons, he felt, must develop " into the
central government which will be the organ
of federating the municipalities." Fabianism
thus implied no central bureaucracy : what it
demanded was partly, indeed, a more efficient
and expert central government (and there is
plenty of room for that), but primarily an expert
local civil service, in close touch with and under
the control of a really democratic municipal
government. It is difficult to say that this is
bureaucracy, or that it is not desirable. Many
men who are not Fabians or Socialists of any
kind feel strongly that the breathing of more
vigour and interest into local politics, and the

erection of a proper local civil service, are the great problems of the future.

The policy of Fabianism has thus been somewhat as follows. An intellectual circle has sought to permeate all classes, from the top to the bottom, with a common opinion in favour of social control of socially created values. Resolved to permeate all classes, it has not preached class-consciousness; it has worked as much with and through Liberal " capitalists " as with and through Labour representatives. Resolved gradually to permeate, it has not been revolutionary : it has relied on the slow growth of opinion. Reformist rather than revolutionary, it has explained the impossibility of the sudden " revolution " of the working classes against capital : it has urged the necessity of a gradual amelioration of social conditions by a gradual assertion of social control over unearned increment. Hence Fabianism has not adopted the somewhat cold attitude of the pure Socialist party to Trade Unions, but has rather found in their gradual conquest of better wages and better conditions for the workers the line of social advance congenial with its own principles. Again, it has preached that the society which is to exert control must be democratic, if the control is to be, as it must be, self-control : it has taught that such democratic self-control must primarily be exerted in democratic local self-government : it has emphasised the need of reconciling democratic control with expert guidance. While it has never advocated " direct action " or the avoidance of political activity, while on the contrary it has advocated the conquest of

social reforms on the fields of parliamentary
and municipal government, it has not defended
the State as it is, but has rather urged the need
for a state which is based on democracy tempered by respect for the " expert." In this way
Socialism of the Fabian type has made representative democracy its creed.   It has adopted
the sound position, that democracy flourishes
best in that form of State, in which the people
freely produce, thanks to an equality of educational opportunity, and freely choose, thanks to
a wide and active suffrage, their own best members for their guidance, and, since they have
freely produced and chosen them, give them
freely and fully the honour of their trust.   And
thus Socialists like Mr. Sidney Webb and Mr.
Ramsay Macdonald have not coquetted with
primary democracy, which has always had a
magnetic attraction for Socialists.   The doctrine that the people itself governs directly
through obedient agents—the doctrine of
mandate and plebiscite, of referendum and
initiative—is not the doctrine of the best
English Socialism.   Mr. Webb's *Industrial
Democracy* shows how Trade Unions, in
groping towards the best scheme of government for themselves, have advanced from
attempts at primary self-government, which
failed, to a policy of government through
elected representatives, which has succeeded :
Mr. Ramsay Macdonald's *Socialism and Government* (1909) is a strong and cogent plea for
representative democracy against the claims of
mandate and referendum, and even against
proportional representation, so far as advocacy
of proportional representation is based on the

view that Parliament is only intended to serve as a mirror of national opinion.

Behind both the economics and the politics of the type of Socialism which we have been discussing there lies an organic theory of society. Economically, society is conceived as a living body which co-operates with the individual in the creation of wealth. We are not really each the architect of our own fortune, as we appear to be. We have all a coadjutor; and that coadjutor is the society in which we live, which is perpetually creating social values partly by its mere growth, as when the extension of a town adds a new value to urban land, but still more by its own manifold activities of education and administration. Politically again society is an organic unity, with a real " general will " of its own such as Rousseau conceived, a general will which has to express itself, not as Rousseau held, in a direct and primary assembly of all the citizens, but through the channels of a purified system of representation. In advocating the conception of a social organism Mr. Ramsay Macdonald, the representative of what may be called biological Socialism, naturally uses biological language. And indeed it is obvious that the analogy of the living organism, so far as it has any value, is of value to Socialism rather than to the individualism advocated by Spencer. " Each for other " is at once the motto of a physical organism and of socialistic doctrine. It is thus logical, as a French critic has remarked, that Mrs. Webb, the disciple of the political philosophy of Herbert Spencer before her conversion to Socialism, has expressly used the metaphor of the social organism against her old master and in defence of the creed he denounced.

The development of Liberalism, during the last few years, shows considerable traces of Fabian influence. Liberal writers like Prof. Hobhouse and Mr. J. A. Hobson [1] have both argued in favour of the intervention of the State in the field of socially created values. Mr. Hobson in particular has urged that the individual is not the only unit of economic production; that the community is itself a producer of values; and that the State, which is the organ of the community, may claim a special right to impose special taxation on such values. The old individualistic view of the State thus seems to be definitely shed by modern Liberalism; and Mr. Hobson, in re-stating the Liberal case, can even enlist the conception of a social organism under its banner. That conception serves to justify the taxation of socially created values, which are argued to be the results of the growth of the organism; and the contention that the State is an organism which feels and thinks, and may claim the right to express its feelings and thoughts, has been applied by Mr. Hobson not only to defend that right to equality of franchise and of representation, which alone will allow the real voice of the whole body to speak, but even to enforce an advocacy of the Referendum.

Collectivism of the Fabian order was the dominant form of Socialism in England till within the last three or four years. *Autres temps, autres mœurs.* A young century, which

[1] See *Democracy and Reaction* (1894), and *The Crisis of Liberalism* (1909).

feels (as we must all have felt) that during the last few years it has been living at a rapid pace, is convinced that it must be novel in order to be up to date. Besides, this is the day of criticism of all the "conventions" of the past—of marriage and divorce, of dress and deportment; and even the advanced Radicalisms of the past are now themselves "conventions" which must be served with a notice to quit in order to make room for new tenants. And so we hear of Mr. Belloc's Distributivism : we are told of Syndicalism : we are presented with Guild-Socialism.

Underlying these novelties there is perhaps one common basis—a general reaction against "the State." One phase of that reaction was considered at the end of a preceding chapter; and it has already been seen in this chapter that there has always been a section of Socialist opinion hostile to political action.[1] This section is now engaged in struggle with the "administrative" Socialism of the Fabian school, and in revolt against its definite recognition of the State as the organ of Socialism. It is urged that the State as an organ of Socialism has two great defects. State-Socialism involves two things—a governing class, and, in the democratic state, an electoral machinery to elect that governing class. The governing class under State-Socialism becomes a bureaucracy, regimenting and controlling the life of the citizen. This inaugurates a "servile" state : it ruins democracy, because "the existence of a governing class is the negation of democracy." Again

[1] Anarchist doctrines were advocated after 1870, in connection with a policy of small communal groups, by adversaries and rivals of Marx, like Bakunin.

the electoral machinery has its defects. A great electorate is liable to be advertisement-drugged and caucus-ridden; and in any case a body of state workers may unite to use their votes in order to put pressure on the State and to secure higher wages and better conditions of employment. Thus State-Socialism means a self-interested electorate partly regimented by, and partly—in reaction—dictating to, a governing bureaucracy.

These are arguments by which the old-fashioned individualist and the neo-socialist are curiously joined and knit together in opposition to collectivist Socialism. And there are other bonds of union. Just as the individualist objects to any discrimination against land and rents, and urges that profits stand on the same footing as rents, being just as much "unearned" and just as much "socially created," so too does the advanced Socialist. The one puts rents and profits on the same footing in order to save both from the Chancellor of the Exchequer: the other puts them on the same footing in order to gain both for "national guilds"; but both are agreed in protesting against the discrimination advocated by the Fabians. Again, there is a certain anti-intellectualism common to individualists and to advanced Socialists. Collectivism means the triumph of the idea of a self-conscious rational organisation of society; it means the direction of the activity of the community in every detail by the reason of the community. The old individualist prefers to trust the empiric instinct of rule of thumb; he leaves each member of the community to follow his own lead, trusting to some final if mysterious reconciling harmony. In a word, he claims all reason for the individual, who knows by reason his own interest, and he leaves none to the community, which, having no guiding reason, must leave its affairs, if it has any, to go their own way. The advanced Socialist tends to anti-intellectualism of a different order. Unlike the individualist, he loves groups rather than individuals; but like the individualist he is not enamoured of the State-group, and like the individualist he does not credit groups with any great amount of reason. He trusts in their instinct, which when the day comes will be adequate to the day's need, but until it comes will not worry itself unduly with thought. This anti-intellectualism is most conspicuous in some of the French Syndicalist theories (which are not altogether the same, it is true, as actual French Syndicalism); but it also appears, for instance, in Mr. Belloc's belief that the Faith will, in some way unexplained, save Europe from being regimented into a servile State—or, in other words, from being guided by mere reason.

In whatever ways advanced Socialism may agree with old individualism, it is of course a very different creed. Both may reject collectivism; but the one rejects it in order not to go forward at all, and the other in order to go much further forward. The general advance is towards the substitution of Occupationalism for Socialism. Instead of control exerted by the whole society, as a body of owners, over itself as a body of workers, control is to be exerted over their members by each occupation or profession. Whether it be termed Syndicalism, or Guild-

H

Socialism, or by other names, the common basis of the new creed seems to be a belief in the economic self-government of the occupation or profession. Mr. Belloc, for instance, advocates in the *Servile State* (1912) Distributivism, by which we are to understand the assignment to every man, as far as possible, of individual private property; but it is the core of his argument that this vastly increased private property will need to be protected, as in the Middle Ages he thinks that it was protected, by co-operative guilds," and " by the autonomy of great artisan corporations."   For unless there are such bodies, imposing voluntary restraints on alienation in order to prevent the rise of an economic oligarchy, and stopping sale by the many in order to prevent purchase by the few, history will repeat itself, and landlordism and capitalism will return again.   Mr. Belloc lays stress mainly on individual property, and he does not emphasise, though he recognises, the need of co-operative association.   The authors of *Guild Socialism* (1914) are exclusively concerned with co-operative association.   They too, like Mr. Belloc, have something of a mediæval ideal; and they unite the mediæval " craft " with the French *syndicat* to produce the new Socialism.   Under their plan the State indeed owns the means of production; but the guild, as trustee, controls their use.   The guild employs itself : the guild determines its wages, its hours, its conditions of labour, the prices of its product.   Such a guild, it is urged, will mean the real application of democracy to industry, which will by its means be voluntarily organised and freely directed; while State-

Socialism can only mean the application of
bureaucracy, which is, in the issue, the negation
of democracy.

The mediæval State, we are often told, was a
" community of communities," a sum of corporate bodies—guilds and monasteries, boroughs
and shires. Under Guild-Socialism the modern
State will be a community of professional
guilds. But the State will be more than a sum
of such guilds. It will not be a mere bracket
or hyphen, but a real entity in itself. It is
on this point that Guild-Socialism parts company with Syndicalism, which on the whole is
a French, and not an English school of thought.
Syndicalists, intent on the perfect autonomy of
the professional group, have gone to war against
the State. They have held *patrie* and *propriété*
to be convertible terms; they have urged that
the State protects property, and that the State
must be destroyed in order to destroy property.
La classe, c'est la patrie, has been their motto;
they have sought to substitute occupationalism
for patriotism. The authors of *Guild Socialism,*
on the contrary, find room for the State as well
as the guild; and this they do by a " separation
of powers," which seems *prima facie* simple,
though in the issue it would prove sufficiently
difficult. To the State they would assign all
matters that concern the national soul—fine
art, education, international relations, justice,
public conduct; for the guild they would
vindicate all matters that concern the national
income. To the State, for instance, is reserved
all higher education : to the guilds is left all
the sphere of technical education. Thus will be
realised in the State the two democracies—the

economic and the political; and the two
democracies are the vital and necessary condition of any democracy at all. For unless
there be economic democracy—the control by
the workers themselves of their work—political
democracy is all in vain. It is an idle thing that
a man should have a vote in the affairs of the
State unless he has already a voice in the affairs
of the guild : " economic power precedes and
controls political power." Once establish the
democratic guild, and all other things will be
added. A State will arise which is the owner
of all the means of production, but lets such
means to the guilds on condition that they
pay for their charter an annual rent; and
these rents will provide the State with all its
finances. Such a State, with no anxiety about
its finances, and with no concern for economic
affairs, which will either be controlled by each
guild separately or, for the larger and more
common issues, by a conference of guilds, will
turn itself freely to the things of the spirit, and
live its own life " certainly independent, probably even supreme." And if we ask, " What
is to happen if guild quarrels with guild, each
trying to get the best conditions for its own
members ? What is to happen if the Conference of the Guilds, with its own policy and its
own feeling, quarrels with the parliament of
the State ? " we must content ourselves, as
Montesquieu sought to content himself when
he thought of the possibility of struggles arising
from the separation of powers, by the thought
that " since by the natural movement of things
they are forced to move, they will move together."

In truth, any doctrine of separation of powers, such as Guild-Socialism advocates, is bound to collapse before the simple fact of the vital interdependence of all the activities of the " great society " of to-day. The State is one body : no clever essay in dichotomy can get away from that fact. In vain do you assign international relations to the State, and the control of economic production to the guild : international relations involve questions of economic production, and questions of economic production involve international relations. Either the State must go, as Syndicalists seem to advocate, and that means chaos, or the State must remain—and then, if you are to have Socialism, it must be State-Socialism. If there is to be a State, it must have the final responsibility for the life of its citizens. Nevertheless, State-Socialism may have its lessons to learn from Guild-Socialism. It is interesting to see how Mr. Graham Wallas, one of the authors of the *Fabian Essays* of 1889, brings a fresh and receptive mind to bear on the new suggestions in his latest work, *The Great Society* (1914).

A quarter of a century ago the Fabians, assuming the State as it stood, though desiring a more fully democratic structure of its central parliament and its local representative bodies, urged that this State should gradually assume the control of economic life. Representative democracy and State-control of production were its two interconnected tenets ; but assuming that representative democracy would come, and come rapidly, of itself, Fabians concentrated their attention on the means of introducing State-control of production. Mr. Wells, in *New Worlds for Old* (1908), sought to bring back attention to problems of government, and suggested that the structure of government was a problem prior to the socialisation of industry. " Before you can transfer property from private to collective control you must have something in the way of a governing institution which has a reasonably good chance of developing into an efficient controlling body." Mr. Wells seems to suggest new local areas of administration and new types of electorate ; but his main insistence is on the study of social psychology in order to discover the areas and electorates which will produce the most vigorous " collective mind," and thus provide the necessary organ of any collectivist State. Mr. Wallas, a member of the London County Council for many years, has had actual experience of local areas and of the behaviour of electorates, while the study of social psychology, as we have already seen, has found in him one of its most original exponents. In both ways he has been led to face the problem, stated by Mr. Wells, of " the scientific reconstruction of our representative and ad-ministrative machinery so as to give power and real expression to the developing collective mind of the community."

The *Great Society* of Mr. Wallas is not, like *Guild Socialism*, an ambitious attempt to find new cadres for the " communal mind." It is rather a treatise on social therapeutics—or, if one may use a clumsy word, social psycho-therapeutics. Its author seeks in the light of social psychology—which is " the knowledge which will enable us to forecast and therefore to influence the conduct of large numbers of human beings organised in societies "—to diagnose the diseases of our present system of representative government and to suggest their remedies. Diseases there are, he admits, which the Fabians of 1889 did not foresee, but which further experience of political life and the new study of social psychology have since 1889 combined to discover. There is the whole process of hypnotising the electorate by every manner of " suggestion "; there is manipulation of the electorate by great interests for their own ends; there is the tendency of certain classes of electors to use their voting power to put pressure on the government or municipality which is their employer. Syndicalism, in its various phases, is an attempt to correct these evils. Flying from geographical areas—municipalities, counties, constituencies—it would find in the non-local association of the organised profession the line of that " reconstruction " which Mr. Wells desires. But guilds too may have their diseases : in the Middle Ages they certainly had; and to-day also a Socialism based on guilds might mean a spirit of exclusive monopoly, a spirit of jealousy between guild and guild, a spirit of pettiness which preferred the small association to the great society in which it lives. A *via media* has thus to be found between State-Socialism based on local representation, and Guild-Socialism based on the principle of profession; and it is in a retention of collectivism and representation, tempered and modified by recognition of groups, and by the institution of new authorities free from liability to pressure, that Mr. Wallas seeks this *via media.* He would, for instance, recognise the group in the constitution of the Second Chamber, while reserving the geographical electorate for the Lower Chamber. He would advocate the creation of bodies, with a majority of elected representatives, but with a minority of members appointed by professional organisations, for the control of undertakings, educational or economic, in which the unqualified use of elected representatives might lead to manipulation or pressure, while on the other hand the unqualified use of professional management might breed exclusiveness and monopoly. In a word, he seeks to reconcile Fabianism with Professionalism in much the same way, though with more clarity and logic, as the British Socialist Party in 1912 attempted to reconcile Marxianism with Trade Unionism.

Socialism thus presents to-day a number of strands of thought, some of which, if distinct, are difficult to distinguish, and some of which are being tied and twisted together in efforts at mediation and reconciliation. There is the Marxian tradition which lives in the Socialist party proper; there is the tradition of the Webbs which lives in Fabianism. Both are forms of State-Socialism, with differences which we have already seen, but with this great common factor that they recognise the " great society " as the organ of Socialism. On the other hand there are the new doctrines of Syndicalism and Guild-Socialism, which differ fundamentally from the old tradition in adopting professional groups as the organ of Socialism, and in that respect are essentially

similar, but which differ from one another in
their attitude to the State. Here are some
four strands; and of these the Marxian seems
to be seeking a connection with the Syndicalist,
to judge by the tone of the British Socialist
Party in 1912, while the Fabian, to judge from
Mr. Wallas, is not altogether averse from the
strand of Guild-Socialism. Such an expression
of a complicated situation is, of course, artifi-
cially simple. What is clear is that the idea
of the guild—whether, as with Mr. Belloc, it is
only the shield and cover of peasant proprietor-
ship, or, as with the authors of *Guild Socialism*,
the essential organisation of a life in which
the guild fills and permeates the whole mind—
is the idea of the hour. The criticism of State-
Socialism which proceeds from this idea is
likely to lead to a new adjustment of Socialist
theory. When it is urged that the old Socialism
is just Capitalism " writ large," with the officials
of the State replacing the managers of Capitalism, but with " wagery " still left as the condition of the ordinary citizen, the thrust goes
home. After all, Socialism which works through
the great society cannot avoid its Scylla and
Charybdis. Either it must evolve a great and
independent administration, which will control
the lives of its citizens—and that way, it may
be urged, lies status and the servile State; or
it must evolve a great and sovereign electorate,
which will control the action of the administration—and that way lies a fierce tussle of competition between different classes of State-
employees to decide which shall put the
greater pressure on the administration, a competition ending in the anarchic State. There

H 2

is, indeed, no guarantee that the guild will
avoid Charybdis, or that the struggle between
guild and guild will not mean competition and
anarchy. But the guild has in its favour that
federalistic trend of thought which, as has
already been seen, is powerful in modern
thought. The High Churchman, concerned for
the independent life of the ecclesiastical group,
finds the teaching of the Guild-Socialists a not
unwelcome ally; he may, in an expansive
moment, declare that he too is a Syndicalist.
The political movement towards the recognition of the rights of national groups, conspicuous alike in our own recent politics and in the
present politics of a warring Europe, sets the
same way. And finally, perhaps most important of all, there has to be taken into
consideration, over and above federalistic
tendencies of Churchmen or of politicians, that
growth of voluntary co-operation, particularly
in the field of agriculture, which has been at
work, especially in Ireland, for some years
past. Agricultural industry has not, indeed,
become a guild; but it has gone some way
towards becoming a sphere of voluntary and
self-managed co-operation. And thus it would
seem to follow that, if we cannot dispense with
State-control of economic life, as guild-Socialists
seem to think, neither can we dispense with
guild-management of such life, as State-
Socialists used to believe. The problem to be
solved is the reconciliation of State-control
with voluntary co-operation. That problem
cannot be solved by a division of functions
which would leave the State no control of
economic life; but neither can it be solved by

a concentration of powers which would, at
any rate in the great staple industries, leave
voluntary co-operation no room.

On the literature devoted to the criticism
of Socialism we cannot here touch. In 1908
Mr. Mallock published a *Critical Examination
of Socialism,* and Mr. Arnold Foster a statement of *The Case against Socialism.* Mr.
Donisthorpe, nearly twenty years before, in
various pamphlets written for the Liberty and
Property Defence League, had preached in-
cisively the gospel of " Let Be." In his hands,
and in the hands of Auberon Herbert, a stout
individualist who sought to confine the State
to the administration of justice, and to sub-
tract from its scope everything except the
defence of person and property, the reaction
against any form of paternalism runs to the
length of an interesting if academic anarchism.

There is one work, however, which is hardly
a criticism of socialistic doctrine, but rather a
pathetic analysis of socialistic tendencies in
actual life, whose charm demands some notice.
This is Pearson's *National Life and Character*
(1894). Anticipating, with regret but also
with resignation, the cessation of all progress
and the coming of a stationary State, partly
owing to the pressure of the lower races upon
the higher, partly owing to socialistic tendencies which this pressure will strengthen,
Pearson calmly analyses the character of this
stationary State. Fundamentally, he feels, it
will mean a dependent reliance on the State
which will check all outbursts of originality.
The State will give its members education,
health, employment and all manner of placid

security. The State will become their cult;
the hold of Churches on their members will
grow weak, and the appeal of families to their
members will grow faint. " The decay of the
family " forms the subject of one of his most
striking chapters. But Pearson had hardly
reckoned with the fundamental vitality of
those associations within the State—Church
and union and guild as well as family—which
are again to-day asserting their rights of existence. In 1832 men feared that an encroaching
State would engulf the Church; and yet within
a year the Church was asserting through New-
man, and has asserted ever since, its own
rights to an independent existence. And in
like manner, though in 1894 Pearson may have
anticipated that an implacably expanding
State would absorb all human life, by 1914
the current of thought seems to be setting the
other way.

Yet there is one of Pearson's anticipations
which, while it runs athwart what seems to be
the main current of the internal development
of contemporary England, is nevertheless confirmed, to all appearances, by the general
tendency of Europe at large. He anticipated
that though Socialism in its militant stage
might be international and even anti-national,
and though again it might be anti-militarist,
yet Socialism once triumphant might become,
and would tend to become, in defence of itself
and its own achievement, severely national,
possibly protectionist, and almost certainly
militarist. A Socialist State, he felt, could not
run the risk of having its own standard of life
debased by the competition of inferior States,

and in self-defence it would don all the panoply of exclusion. The tendencies of some of the most advanced democracies of our own Empire seem rather to corroborate than to invalidate this thesis. And the extent to which the Socialists of Europe have lately sprung to arms in defence of their national States, even before the days of the victory of their cause, seems to suggest that the triumph of Socialism would not necessarily be the triumph of internationalism.

We have considered the bearing of economic theory on the general conception of the internal polity and function of the State; it remains to consider its bearing on the theory and practice of international relations. Free Trade, the cardinal tenet of the old political economy, not only issued in a political theory of laissez-faire in domestic affairs; it also issued in a correlative theory of non-intervention in the field of foreign policy. It was the argument of Cobden that Free Trade demanded a comity of nations, animated by a cosmopolitan ideal, as the necessary condition of that peaceful interchange of commodities which alone can produce the maximum of wealth. He thanked God "that Englishmen live in a time when it is impossible to make war profitable." Spiritual motives contributed to determine this attitude. Cobden, like Bright, had a genuine detestation of war; and the ideals of pacificism and cosmopolitanism which he cherished were backed by a moral appeal to the conscience as well as by a pecuniary appeal to the pocket. In Green's conception of war as in its nature morally wrong, and in

his cognate conception of a " universal brotherhood " of humanity, we may trace the purest
presentation of this moral appeal. Green had
come under the influence of Bright; and he
shows that influence at its best. But it is
none the less true that the Cobdenite interpretation of life was rather economic than
moral. Everything was made to hinge on the
economic sentiment of the individual; little
or no regard was paid to the national sentiment of the organised State. Economy was
the criterion of politics; policy was good or
bad, as it promoted or hindered the maximum
of production; there was little conception of
any national duty to intervene either internally
on behalf of depressed classes, or externally
on behalf of struggling causes.

Something of a change came with Gladstone.
He might have little zest for the cause of social
reform, and little comprehension of the need
of internal intervention; but on the foreign
policy of England he left a decisive impression.
He had caught the great faith of Mazzini, that
" nation is mission "; he felt that it was the
duty of a nation to take its stand in the world
of European politics, and to lend its sympathy,
if not its aid, to struggling causes and oppressed
nationalities. If he left no great or striking
achievement, he bequeathed a tradition; he
identified the name of England abroad with
a policy of sympathetic intervention in favour
of Liberal and national causes, and he weaned
his own party at home from the cult of a foreign
policy springing solely from economic motives
and issuing only in non-intervention. While a
change of this nature may be traced in England,

another and far greater change was being accomplished in Germany. Germany became the apostle of the creed of national self-sufficiency. To the cosmopolitan ideal of Cobden she opposed the nationalist ideal of List. The four-square nation, encouraging every side of its economic life by a system of scientific protection, and claiming from all its citizens, for the perfection of its national ideal, a complete and unswerving loyalty, threw a gage of defiance to all visionary dreams of a denationalised world. To Treitschke, as to Mazzini, " nation is mission "; but to Treit-schke the mission of a nation is the extension of national culture, and—since power is the vehicle of culture—the extension of national power.

In days such as these Mr. Norman Angell recurs to Cobdenism. If Cobden thanked God that England could not make a war profitable, the author of *The Great Illusion* (1909) seeks to extend the scope of his gratitude, and to prove that no nation can make a war profitable. He brings to the argument not only the science of economics, but the sciences of biology and psychology. By the aid of biology he seeks to refute the militarist appeal to the doctrine of natural selection. War, it is true, selects the fittest, but it selects them for destruction. By the aid of psychology he seeks to refute the militarist appeal to the unchanging pug-nacity of human nature. It is true that human nature does not change; but at any rate it reacts in new ways on new environments, and its reaction on the environment of the modern world is a lively sense of the profitableness of peace. But the fundamental basis of Mr. Norman Angell's argument is economic. He adopts the individualism of the old economics, and is as blind as the Benthamites to the fact of nationalism. He adopts the isolation and exaggeration of the economic motive which characterised the old economics, and supports the cause of pacificism, like Cobden, by the *argumentum ad crumenam.* But he differs from the older economists in selecting for emphasis a different set of economic factors. They had laid stress on the interdependence of the world's markets. He lays stress on the interdependence of the world's banks and Stock Exchanges.

The primary fact from which Mr. Angell starts is the fact of " a synchronised bank-rate the world over and reacting bourses." Improved means of communication, and especially the telegraph, have created a single system of credit for all the world; and that system is so delicately interwoven, and so finely intermeshed, that a nation can never gain profit, even if it gains victory, by throwing the sword into its texture. The one sure and certain result of drawing the sword is the disturbance of credit—the credit of the nation which draws the sword no less than that of the rest. " The telegraph and the bank have rendered military force economically futile." The old argument of diplomacy ran somewhat as follows : " The growth of industry involves new markets; the acquisition of new markets involves control of transport; the control of transport, for overseas markets, involves a navy; the navy involves, in the last resort, war." Mr. Angell counters with a new argument. "The telegraph involves a single system of credit for the civilised world; that system of credit involves the financial interdependence of all States; that financial interdependence involves peace." To rest the cause of peace on the one foundation of banking may seem precarious. Banking is only one of many economic activities; and it is in many respects peculiar. It has been international for centuries; Italian bankers financed our English kings in their struggles with France in the fourteenth century; but none the less wars and rumours of wars have never ceased. It is on banking, nevertheless, that Mr. Angell rests his case; and it is only by way of a supplement, and almost of an afterthought, that he draws new arguments for the cause of peace from the international organisation to which Capital and Labour are both tending. "In banking"—his argument seems to run—" and for that matter in other economic things also, the world is one society. Politically, it is several distinct societies tending to compete with one another. Of these two facts the former is the more important, and determines action to a greater extent. It pays men better to think and feel as members of the universal economic society, whose attribute is peace, than to think and feel as members of limited political societies, whose attribute is war. The pocket is the rudder of human nature; and therefore, as soon as they realise this fact, men will cease from war."

This is not the place to enter into any discussion of Mr. Angell's economics. Our concern lies with the political theory which they involve. That theory, it is obvious from what has been said, is necessarily loaded by a bias against the State. Mr. Norman Angell is one of the many contemporary forces which make for the discrediting of the State. He is " against the government." He speaks of " the irrationalism of the mob-mind "—" the fact that a man will in politics, in a matter where patriotism is involved, act with an irrationalism and an absence of any sense of responsibility, which he would never display in the conduct of his private business." Here we catch a new strain in that anti-intellectualist reaction against the State and all its works which is so dominant in modern theory. We seem to listen to a financier sadly reflecting, as he compares the State with his well-managed office, *quantula sapientia gubernatur mundus.* But well or ill governed, the State is to Mr. Angell only a piece of political mechanism. The only thing predicated in the conception of the State is particular administrative conditions : modern State divisions represent mere administrative convenience. One can hardly recognise a State which has sunk to an administrative area; and it is easy for Mr. Angell, when he has once begun to see the State through the wrong end of the telescope, to deny that it possesses any real existence. The State, he argues, is not a single body or " homogeneous personality." To ascribe any personality, or will, or responsibility to the State is a delusion, partly due to the survival of ideas which may have had their place in the time of Aristotle, but are now outgrown as a result of economic evolution—partly due to a false analogy between the State and the individual. A modern State is not a single life, or a single conception of life; it contains within itself many conceptions of life, some of them mutually exclusive, and some of them (as, for instance, the Catholic conception) " agreeing absolutely with conceptions in foreign States." Having decomposed the State into a loose federation of groups, Mr. Angell naturally denies not only that it is a personality, or that it can undertake responsibility, but even that it has any real national feeling. " The formation of States has disregarded national divisions altogether." From the examples which he gives it would appear that Mr. Angell really means " racial " when he says " national "; and while it may be conceded to him that modern States are not racially homogeneous, it cannot be equally conceded that the absence of such homogeneity demonstrates the absence of nationality, or proves that nationality cannot stand in the way of economic co-operation between States.

So far we have dealt with the negative side of Mr. Angell's political theory. It has also its positive aspect. He admits that men really are united by a community of feeling; but he urges that that community is not defined by geographical limits or administrative areas. Men are united by a common feeling of economic interest, which is irrespective of such limits and areas : they are united, again, by the common feeling of their profession, or their class, which is equally non-geographical and non-political. What unites men is a concep-

tion of life; and the real " psychic " divisions
are not between nations, but between opposing
conceptions of life—not between political
frontiers, but between political philosophies.
In one passage where he confesses that he
regards " certain English conceptions of life
bearing on matters of law, and social habit,
and political philosophy, as infinitely preferable
to the German," Mr. Angell seems, somewhat
inconsistently, to admit that each State is,
or has, a conception of life. Elsewhere, and
more consistently, he identifies conceptions of
life with political parties. Germany is not
opposed to England; but in Germany and in
England democracy is opposed to autocracy,
and Socialism is opposed to individualism. In
a word parties, which are supposed by Mr.
Angell to be, but as a matter of fact never are,
the same in all countries, are the fundamental
groupings or conceptions of life which constitute the real psychic communities. Further,
these parties are conceived to be primarily
representative of different conceptions of life
in one particular field—the field of social conflict. The problems of such conflict are " much
more profound and fundamental than any
conception which coincides or can be identified
with State divisions." The ultimate upshot
of Mr. Angell's doctrine is plain. He banishes
the conflict of States in order to set in its
place the conflict between international parties
espousing different sides in the social conflict.
That is to say, he banishes one kind of war in
favour of a worse kind of war. Social struggles are always the bitterest of struggles; and
social struggles waged by international parties

would be the bitterest of social struggles. Mr.
Angell seems to think that a social struggle is
justified by being international. If a social
struggle is ever to be condemned, it is most
to be condemned when it is international.

It is exactly the struggle of classes which the
State serves, if not to prevent, at any rate to
keep within limits. The value of the State lies
in the fact that it supplies a common substance
for man's interest and devotion, in which the
competing claims of class and of party can be
reconciled. The government of the State
adjusts the claim of classes to one another,
creating in the process social rights; at the
very least, it keeps the ring as a neutral referee,
inducing competing parties to obey the rules of
the game. But the State itself is above the
government; and it is more than " particular
administrative conditions." It is the common
substance in which very different elements are
so firmly knit together, that they can rejoice
in their membership. It is in vain to speak of
" the blind dogma of patriotism," or to seek to
eliminate nationalism. The State, after all,
is a single conception of life, as Mr. Angell himself incidentally admits : it is a single conception which can blend and contain a number of
other conceptions and a variety of other groups.
That conception, which the Germans call
" culture," is the parent of patriotism : that
conception, again, constitutes the Nation. Far
from being weak, it is only too strong. It has
its peculiar home in Germany, and in the
teaching of Treitschke. But since the campaign
in Tripoli, it has found new vogue in Italy ; and
in the form of imperialism, and in alliance with

the idea of a national " vocation " to spread ᴀ
national type, it is by no means unknown in
England. It has vitally affected the recent
development of Socialism. Socialists, long
attracted by the idea of internationalism, seem
nowadays, alike in France and Germany, to
have turned their faces to the rising sun of
Nationalism.

The fact of international economics, so much
emphasised by Mr. Angell, is in many respects, if
not so absolutely as he conceives, a fact of vital
importance. The fact of national politics, which
he seeks to eliminate, is equally, or even more,
a true and vital fact. Economic progress has
outrun political structure. We cannot, however, bring the two into line at the cost of
suppressing one of the elements. We must all
seek to be internationalists, because that is the
highest ideal which we can discern. A true
internationalism, however, must perhaps differ
from that of Mr. Angell in two fundamental
respects. In the first place, it must recognise
the existence of the State in all its fulness, and
it must seek to comprehend states in its fold
without any derogation from the fulness of
their being. In the second place, it must base
itself not on the economic appeal to the individual, and not on the argument that it pays,
but rather on the moral appeal to national
conscience, and on the argument that it is right
to conceive the relations of states as compre-
hended in the sphere of a common and public
law of the nations. There is, as we have seen
in an earlier chapter, a sense of right common to
civilised nations. It is in the explication of
that sense, and in its translation into a concrete

legal embodiment, that the hope of internationalism lies. Internationalism must pursue a legal development, not based on (though it may be aided by) economic facts, but based (as all legal development is based) on a sense of right inherent in a common conscience—the common conscience of the civilised world. An extension of extradition treaties; an extension of the Hague Tribunal and the reference of disputes between states to that Tribunal; an extension of international treaties to include limitation of armaments—such are the ways which international development may be expected to take. Of such a development, resting on such a basis, Lord Haldane spoke in 1913 in an address to the American Bar Association. And it is on such a development, taking a legal form, and resting ultimately, as he urged, on the *Sittlichkeit*, or sense of a common ethic, of a group of allied nations, rather than on a development issuing from any economic factor, that we must fix our hopes. Not the abolition of national political structure, but the evolution of forms of international political structure, must be our aspiration and endeavour.

When all criticisms are spent, it remains to express a debt of gratitude to Mr. Angell. He belongs to the cause of internationalism—the greatest of all the causes to which a man can set his hands in these days. The cause will not triumph by economics. But it cannot reject any ally. And if the economic appeal is not final, it has its weight. " We shall perish of hunger," it has been said, " in order to have success in murder." To those who have ears for that saying it cannot be said too often.

EPILOGUE

THE position of political thought in England in 1914 is one of considerable interest. New sources of thought are sending fresh tributaries to the main stream of theory ; new practical forces are at work to direct or divert its current.

Among the new sources of thought we have to reckon social psychology, the new economics, and the new aspect of legal theory which has been emphasised by Maitland. Social psychology tends to issue in a criticism of the machinery and methods of representative government. Intentionally, or unintentionally, it allies itself with a certain trend of anti-intellectualism which is one of the features of the age. In reaction against what they regard as the false intellectualism of the Utilitarians, and the equally false if very different intellectualism of the Idealists, many of the thinkers of to-day are returning to the cult of instinct, or, at the best, of sub-conscious thought. They find unexpected allies. The new economics, in some of its phases, is also intuitional and anti-intellectual. If social psychology tends to base the State as it is on other than intellectual grounds, Syndicalism is prone to expect that non-intellectual forces will suffice to achieve the State as it should be. Both may find themselves in the issue, however paradoxical the prophecy may seem, the servants of Conservatism. Conservatism, with its appeal to sentiment, and its antipathy to doctrinaire Radicalism, is the residuary legatee of all anti-intellectual movements.

At present, however, the current which sets

against " intellectualism " sets also against the
State. A certain tendency to discredit the
State is now abroad. The forces which combine to spread this tendency are very various.
There is the old doctrine of the natural
rights of man, which lies behind most of the
movements that advocate resistance to the
authority of the State. But there is also the
new doctrine of the rights of groups, which is
to-day a still more potent cause of opposition
to the State. In the sphere of economics this
doctrine assumes the form of Guild-Socialism.
In the sphere of legal theory it assumes the
form of insistence on the real personality, the
spontaneous origin, and (with some of its
exponents) the "inherent rights " of permanent
associations. In this latter form the doctrine
has been urged on the one hand by the advocates of the rights of Trade Unions, and on
the other hand by the champions of the rights
of churches and ecclesiastical bodies. In both
forms it has tended to produce a federalistic
theory of the State, whether the State is regarded as a union of guilds, or as "a community
of communities " which embraces groups not
only economic, but also ecclesiastical and
national. In both forms it has consequently
tended to restrict the activity of the State in
order to safeguard the rights of the group. In
a different form, and from a different point of
view, the theory of Mr. Norman Angell, so far
as it touches the State, shows at once a certain
anti-intellectualism and a definite tendency to
belittle the State in comparison with economic
or social groups.

We may need, and we may be moving towards, a new conception of the State, and more
especially a new conception of sovereignty,
which shall be broad enough to embrace these
new ideas. We may have to regard every
State—not only the federal State proper, but
also the State which professes to be unitary—
as in its nature federal; we may have to
recognise that sovereignty is not single and
indivisible, but multiple and multicellular.
If we do so, there are two cautions to be borne
in mind. In the first place we must be clear
about the intellectual foundations of our new
creed. We must be quite clear what we mean
by our groups ; and we must not content ourselves with a hazy intuition that they are somehow real personalities, or have somehow inherent
rights. It is perhaps possible to find a proper
intellectual vindication for such a creed ; but
until that has been done, the creed will tend
to be lost among those instinctive reactions
against the State, which have helped to give it
vogue, but from which it must be dissociated
in order to become a permanent belief of the
mind. In the second place, we must beware of
the spirit *der stets verneint*. It is natural to
desire to be up-to-date ; it is equally natural
to try to be up-to-date by the use of the facile
method of denial of the obvious and accepted
facts of life. To denounce the servile state
or to castigate the party system is not very
difficult. It is perhaps even easy in an age
that abhors the conventional and admires the
paradoxical. But the State is always with us ;
and the party system, in a State like ours,

which is based on representative government, is
equally inevitable. Where there are representatives, there must be organisation of representatives ; and what organisation there can
be other than party no man has yet discovered.
Sparta has fallen to our lot, and we must adorn
it. The State and its institutions are with us,
and we must make the best of them.

With these provisos, theory may perhaps
safely attempt new excursions into federalism.
It may do so all the more confidently, as the
practical forces at work themselves seem
federalistic. The State in England is seeking,
by Home Rule and Welsh Disestablishment
Bills, to meet the claims of national groups.
All Europe is convulsed with a struggle of
which one object at any rate is a re-grouping of
men in ways which will fulfil national ideals
and accord with national aspirations. Trade
Unions have recovered from Parliament more
than the ground they have lost in the law
courts. The claims of religious groups, in the
field of education, are more and more re-
spected ; and there is less and less reason for
apprehending the tyranny of a " lay " State.
These are the signs of the times ; and speculation has a way of accommodating itself to the
signs. In due time we may expect that theory
will be squared more closely to fact. It will
cease to be belied by the facts ; it will also cease
to deny the facts. But then political theory
would be dead if it were quite true, and quite
obviously true. It grows on the uncertainty of
human affairs ; it thrives on the inadequacy of
its own successive attempts to explain them.

BIBLIOGRAPHY

THE following is not a list of the best books. Indeed some of the books mentioned may be said to be bad books. It has been the writer's purpose to select those books which influenced in their day, or may serve to illustrate to-day, the progress of political thought.

CHAPTERS II. AND III.

T. H. GREEN : *Principles of Political Obligation*, and the lectures on *Liberal Legislation and Freedom of Contract* and on *The English Commonwealth* in his collected works, Vol. III. F. H. BRADLEY : *Ethical Studies* (especially the chapter entitled " My Station and its Duties "). B. BOSANQUET : *Philosophical Theory of the State* (second edition). W. WALLACE : *Lectures and Essays* (especially Part II., Essays i., vii., viii., ix.). J. MACCUNN : *Ethics of Citizenship* and *Six Radical Thinkers.* J. S. MACKENZIE : *An Introduction to Social Philosophy.* J. H. MUIRHEAD : *The Service of the State* (four lectures on the political teaching of T. H. Green). SIR HENRY JONES : *The Working Faith of the Social Reformer.*

CHAPTER IV.

HERBERT SPENCER : *Social Studies* (the original edition of 1851, or the American reprints of that edition, should be used : the edition of 1892 is "edited and abridged "); *Essays* (on the *Social Organism, Specialised Administration,* etc.); *The Study of Sociology; The Principles of Sociology* (see also *Descriptive Sociology*, a great collection of sociological data started by Spencer); *The Man versus The State*; and *The Principles of Ethics,* Part IV. (also printed separately under the title of *Justice*), in which Spencer treats again the subject-matter of *Social Statics.*

D. DUNCAN'S *Life and Letters of H. Spencer* contains a valuable essay by Spencer on *The Filiation of Ideas*, in which he traces the growth of his own thought. F. W. MAITLAND, *Collected Papers,* I. pp. 247–303, discusses Spencer's theory of Society, which is also criticised in D. G. Ritchie's *Principles of State Interference.*

Somewhat analogous in their point of view to Spencer's anarchic individualism are the following : *A Plea for Liberty*, a volume of essays (including essays by Spencer, Donisthorpe and Herbert) edited by T. Mackay; AUBERON HERBERT'S *The Right and Wrong of Compulsion by the State*; and WORDSWORTH DONISTHORPE'S *Individualism : a System of Politics.*

CHAPTER V.

1. The application of biology to politics may be seen in different ways in the following : T. H. HUXLEY : *Methods*

252

and Results and *Ethics and Evolution*. B. KIDD : *Social Evolution* (which may be compared with H. T. BUCKLE's *History of Civilisation*). W. K. CLIFFORD : *Lectures and Essays*, II. 106–176. LESLIE STEPHEN : *Science of Ethics*. S. ALEXANDER : *Moral Order and Progress*. L. T. HOBHOUSE : *Democracy and Reaction*. D. G. RITCHIE : *Darwinism and Politics*, and *Principles of State Interference* (see also *Darwin and Hegel* and *Natural Rights*).

2. The application of psychology to politics appears in W. BAGEHOT : *Physics and Politics*. GRAHAM WALLAS : *Human Nature in Politics*. W. MACDOUGALL : *Social Psychology*.

3. For Sociology see F. H. GIDDINGS : *The Principles of Sociology*. Sociology is almost an American subject, and there are numerous works upon it by other American writers, such as Lester F. Ward and E. A. Ross.

CHAPTER VI.

Sir HENRY MAINE : *Ancient Law, Early Law and Custom, Early History of Institutions*, and *Popular Government*. SIR JAMES STEPHEN : *Liberty, Equality, Fraternity*. SIR R. K. WILSON : *The Province of the State*. JETHRO BROWN : *The Austinian Theory of Law* and *Underlying Principles of Modern Legislation*. A. V. DICEY : *The Law of the Constitution* (eighth edition, 1915), and *Law and Opinion in England* (second edition, 1914). [With the former of Dicey's works cf. W. BAGEHOT : *The English Constitution* (with which in turn cf. S. LOW : *The Governance of England*). These works are not written from a legal point of view, but just for that reason they serve to bring out the distinctiveness of that point of view.] LORD BRYCE : *Studies in History and Jurisprudence*. F. W. MAITLAND : *Political Theories of the Middle Age* (introduction) and *Collected Papers*, III. pp. 210–404. J. N. FIGGIS : *Churches in the Modern State* (cf. also his *Divine Right of Kings* (second edition) and *From Gerson to Grotius*). LORD ACTON : *History of Freedom*.

On what may be called Comparative Politics see SIR J. SEELEY : *Introduction to Political Science*. E. A. FREEMAN : *Comparative Politics* and *History of Federal Government*. H. SIDGWICK : *Development of European Polity*.

CHAPTER VII.

T. CARLYLE : *Past and Present, Chartism, Latter-Day Pamphlets, Shooting Niagara*. J. RUSKIN : *A Joy for Ever, Unto This Last, Munera Pulveris, Time and Tide, Fors Clavigera* (see also SIR E. T. COOK : *Life of Ruskin*). M. ARNOLD : *Culture and Anarchy*. W. E. H. LECKY : *Democracy and Liberty*. F. HARRISON : *Order and Progress* (cf. also

R. CONGREVE: *Essays Political, Social and Religious*). LORD MORLEY: *Compromise, Notes on Politics, Miscellanies* (especially the lecture on Machiavelli), and the life of *Rousseau*.

CHAPTER VIII.

On the conflict between Individualism and Socialism see an essay by B. BOSANQUET, in *The Civilization of Christendom*; W. S. MACKECHNIE: *The State and the Individual*; and F. C. MONTAGUE: *The Limits of Individual Liberty*. On the Individualist side may be mentioned—besides J. S. Mill, H. Sidgwick, and several of the writers mentioned above under Chapter IV.—the following: W. S. JEVONS: *The State in Relation to Labour*; H. LEVY: *Economic Liberalism*; F. W. HIRST: *The Manchester School*.

On the Socialist side the literature is large. (1) On the history of Socialism and its theory, see M. BEER: *Geschichte des Sozialismus in England*, and R. C. K. ENSOR: *Modern Socialism*. (2) Various aspects of socialist theory are presented in: H. M. HYNDMAN: *Historical Basis of Socialism in England*. B. SHAW, S. WEBB, and others: *Fabian Essays*. S. WEBB: *History of Trade Unionism* and *Industrial Democracy*. H. G. WELLS: *New Worlds for Old*. G. WALLAS: *The Great Society*. J. R. MACDONALD: *Socialism and Government*, and *Syndicalism*. P. SNOWDEN: *Socialism and Syndicalism*. (3) The approximation of Liberalism to Collectivist ideas may be seen in the various writings of J. A. HOBSON (e. g. *The Crisis of Modern Liberalism*), and in L. T. HOBHOUSE'S *Labour Movement* and *Democracy and Reaction*. (4) The "last novelties" may be found in H. BELLOC: *The Servile State* and *The Party System*. A. ORAGE: *Guild Socialism*. G. H. D. COLE: *The World of Labour*. (5) Criticisms of socialist politics are to be found in the various writings of W. H. MALLOCK (a stern believer in authority, inequality, and deference) such as *Social Equality, Aristocracy and Evolution*, and *The Critical Examination of Socialism*. Mention should also be made of G. LOWES DICKINSON'S *Justice and Liberty*.

The economic case for internationalism is presented in NORMAN ANGELL'S *Great Illusion*. The case is presented from the ethical point of view in T. H. GREEN'S *Principles of Political Obligation*, pp. 154–179, in L. T. HOBHOUSE'S *Democracy and Reaction*, Chapter VIII., and in LORD HALDANE'S address entitled *Higher Nationality*.

On the general history of political thought in the nineteenth century see J. T. MERZ, *History of European Thought in the Nineteenth Century*, Vol. IV.

INDEX